EDUCATIONAL RESEARCH
FOR SOCIAL JUSTICE

DOING QUALITATIVE RESEARCH IN EDUCATIONAL SETTINGS

Series Editor: Pat Sikes

The aim of this series is to provide a range of high quality introductory research methods texts. Each volume focuses, critically, on one particular methodology enabling a detailed yet accessible discussion. All of the contributing authors are established researchers with substantial, practical experience. While every book has its own unique style, each discusses the historical background of the approach, epistemological issues and appropriate uses. They then go on to describe the operationalization of the approach in educational settings drawing upon specific and vivid examples from the authors' own work. The intention is that readers should come away with a level of understanding that enables them to feel sufficiently confident to undertake their own research as well as to critically evaluate other accounts of research using the approach.

Published titles

Morwenna Griffiths: *Educational Research for Social Justice*
Michael Bassey: *Case Study Research in Educational Settings*

EDUCATIONAL RESEARCH FOR SOCIAL JUSTICE

Getting off the fence

Morwenna Griffiths

Open University Press
Buckingham · Philadelphia

Open University Press
Celtic Court
22 Ballmoor
Buckingham
MK18 1XW

email: enquiries@openup.co.uk
world wide web: http://www.openup.co.uk

and
325 Chestnut Street
Philadelphia, PA 19106, USA

First Published 1998

A catalogue record of this book is available from the British Library

ISBN   0 335 19860 0 (hb)   0 335 19859 7 (pb)

Library of Congress Cataloging-in-Publication Data
Griffiths, Morwenna, 1948–
     Educational research for social justice: getting off the fence / Morwenna
Griffiths.
         p.   cm. – (Doing qualitative research in educational settings)
     Includes bibliographical references (p.   ) and index.
     ISBN 0-335-19860-0 (hardbound). – ISBN 0-335-19859-7 (pbk.)
     1. Education–Research–Social aspects.   2. Educational
equalization–Research.   3. Social justice.   I. Title.   II. Series.
LB1028.G687   1998
370′.7′2–dc21   98-16394
                                                                                    CIP

Typeset by Type Study, Scarborough
Printed in Great Britain by Biddles Ltd, Guildford and King's Lynn

Contents

Series editor's preface

I had never realized just how fascinating research was in its own right. I was expecting the research methods course to be boring, difficult and all about statistics but I couldn't have been more wrong. There is so much to consider, so many aspects, so many ways of finding out what's going on, and not just one way of representing it too. I have been really surprised.

(Student taking an MA in Educational Studies)

I never knew that there was so much to research. I thought that you just chose a method, applied it, did your statistical sums and came up with your findings. The reality is more complicated but so much more interesting and meaningful.

(Student taking an MA in Educational Studies)

The best thing for me was being told that qualitative research is 'proper' research – providing it's done properly of course. What goes on in schools is so complex and involves so many different perspectives that I think you often need a qualitative approach to begin to get some idea of what's going on.

(Student taking an MA in Sociology)

I really appreciate hearing about other researchers' experiences of doing research. It was quite a revelation when I first became aware that things don't always go as smoothly as some written accounts seem to suggest. It's really reassuring to hear honest reports: they alert you to pitfalls and problems and things that you might not have thought about.

(Doctoral student)

Comments such as these will be familiar to anyone who has ever taught or taken a course which aims to introduce the range of research approaches available to social scientists in general and those working in educational settings in particular.

The central message that they convey seems to be that the influence of the positivist scientist paradigm is both strong and pervasive, shaping expectations of what constitutes 'proper', 'valid' and 'worthwhile' research. What Barry Troyna wrote in 1994, continues to be the case; namely that:

> There is a view which is already entrenched and circulating widely in the populist circles ... that qualitative research is subjective, value-laden and, therefore, unscientific and invalid, in contrast to quantitative research, which meets the criteria of being objective, value-free, scientific and therefore valid.
>
> (1994: 9)

Within academic and research circles though, where the development of post-modernist and post-structuralist ideas have affected both thinking and research practice, it can be easy to forget what the popular perspective is. This is because, in these communities, qualitative researchers from the range of theoretical standpoints, utilize a variety of methods, approaches, strategies and techniques in the full confidence that their work is rigorous, legitimate and totally justifiable as research. And the process of peer review serves to confirm that confidence.

Recently, however, for those concerned with and involved in research in educational settings, and especially for those engaged in educational research, it seems that the positivist model, using experimental, scientific, quantitative methods, is definitely in the ascendancy once again. Those of us working in England and Wales, go into the new millennium with the government endorsed exhortation to produce evidence-based research which,

> (firstly) demonstrates conclusively that if teachers change their practice from x to y there will be significant and enduring improvement in teaching and learning; and (secondly) has developed an effective method of convincing teachers of the benefits of, and means to, changing from x to y.
>
> (Hargreaves 1996: 5)

If it is to realize its commendable aims of school effectiveness and school improvement, research as portrayed here, demands 'objectivity', experiments and statistical proofs. There is a problem with this requirement though and the essence of it is that educational institutions and the individuals who are involved in and with them are a heterogeneous bunch with different attributes, abilities, aptitudes, aims, values, perspectives, needs and so on. Furthermore these institutions and individuals are located within complex social contexts with all the implications and influences that this entails. On its own, research whose findings can be expressed in mathematical terms is unlikely to be sophisticated enough to sufficiently accommodate and account for the myriad differences that are involved. As one group of prominent educational researchers have noted:

We will argue that schooling does have its troubles. However, we main-
tain that the analysis of the nature and location of these troubles by
the school effectiveness research literature, and in turn those writing
Department for Employment and Education policy off the back of this
research, is oversimplified, misleading and thereby educationally and
politically dangerous (notwithstanding claims of honourable intent).

(Slee *et al.* 1998: 1–9)

There is a need for rigorous research which does not ignore, but rather
addresses, the complexity of the various aspects of schools and schooling:
for research which explores and takes account of different objective experiences and subjective perspectives, and which acknowledges that qualitative
information is essential, both in its own right and also in order to make full
and proper use of quantitative indicators. The *Doing Qualitative Research
in Educational Settings* series of books is based on this fundamental belief.
Thus the overall aims of the series are: to illustrate the potential that particular qualitative approaches have for research in educational settings, and
to consider some of the practicalities involved and issues that are raised
when doing qualitative research so that readers will feel equipped to embark
on research of their own.

At this point it is worth noting that qualitative research is difficult to
define as it means different things at different times and in different contexts.
Having said this Denzin and Lincoln's (1994) generic definition offers a
useful starting point:

Qualitative research is multimethod in focus, involving an interpretive,
naturalistic approach to its subject matter. This means that qualitative
researchers study things in their natural settings, attempting to make
sense of, or interpret, phenomena in terms of the meanings people bring
to them. Qualitative research involves the studied use and collection of
a variety of empirical materials . . . that describe routine and problem-
atic moments and meanings in individuals' lives. Accordingly, qualitative researchers deploy a wide range of interconnected methods,
hoping always to get a better fix on the subject matter at hand.

(Denzin and Lincoln 1994: 2)

The authors contributing to the series are established, well-known
researchers with a wealth of experience on which to draw and all make use
of specific and vivid examples from their own and others' work. A consequence of this use of examples is the way in which each writer conveys a
sense of research being an intensely satisfying and enjoyable activity, in spite
of the specific difficulties that are sometimes encountered.

Whilst they differ in terms of structure and layout each book deals with:

• The historical background of the approach: how it developed; examples
of its use; implications for its use at the present time.

- Epistemological issues: the nature of the data produced; the roles of the researcher and the researched.
- Appropriate uses: in what research contexts and for which research questions is the approach most appropriate; where might the research be inappropriate or unlikely to yield the best data.

They then describe it and discuss using the approach in educational settings, looking at such matters as:

- How to do it: designing and setting up the research; planning and preparation; negotiating access; likely problems; technical details; recording of data.
- Ethical considerations: the roles of and the relationship between the researcher and the researched; ownership of data; issues of honesty.
- Data analysis.
- Presentation of findings: issues to do with writing up and presenting findings.

Morwenna Griffiths' book *Educational Research for Social Justice: Getting off the fence* goes straight to the heart of questions about 'objectivity', bias, partisanship and the value of 'committed' research. These are questions which are central to critiques of qualitative research per se but which are voiced especially forcefully when it is qualitative research relating in some way to social justice which is at issue. Morwenna's concern is specifically with research which is *for* social justice. This is research where power relations (in particular, those between researcher and researched, between research sponsor, researcher and researched, between writer and reader of research accounts) are immanent and, according to Morwenna, awareness of the implications of this must guide all stages of the design, conduct and reporting of the research. To this end she offers a series of principles to aid those involved in research for social justice in educational institutions. These principles were developed in the course of collaborative work with researcher and teacher-researcher colleagues.

Morwenna's work is influenced by post-modernist ideas. In the context of research which is for social justice, questions of interpretation, of social positioning and of the construction of values and knowledge, are clearly important. Post-modern thinking can offer some useful insights into the implications these areas can have for researchers.

In short, *Educational Research for Social Justice: Getting off the fence* provides a reflective, critical, practical and encouraging source book for any researcher who may be thinking of getting off the fence and getting on with committed research for social justice.

Final note

It was Barry Troyna who initially came up with the idea for this series. Although his publishing career was extensive, Barry had never been a series editor and, in his inimitable way, was very keen to become one. Whilst he was probably best known for his work in the field of 'race', Barry was getting increasingly interested in issues to do with methodology when he became ill with the cancer which was eventually to kill him. It was during the twelve months of his illness that he and I drew up a proposal and approached potential authors. All of us knew that it was very likely that he would not live to see the series in print but he was adamant that it should go ahead, nonetheless. The series is, therefore, something of a memorial to him and royalties from it will be going to the Radiotherapy Unit at the Walsgrave Hospital in Coventry.

Pat Sikes

References

Denzin, N. and Lincoln, Y. (1994) Introduction: entering the field of qualitative research. In N. Denzin and Y. Lincoln (eds) *Handbook of Qualitative Research*. California: Sage.

Hargreaves, D. (1996) Teaching as a research-based profession: possibilities and prospects. Teacher Training Agency Annual Lecture. London: TTA.

Slee, R. and Weiner, G. with Tomlinson, S. (eds) (1998) Introduction: school effectiveness for whom? In *School Effectiveness for Whom? Challenges to the School Effectiveness and School Improvement Movements*. London: Falmer.

Troyna, B. (1994) Blind faith? Empowerment and educational research, *International Studies in the Sociology of Education*, 4(1): 3–24.

Acknowledgements

I owe more than I can say to a large number of people who have contributed directly and indirectly to my writing this book. I want to acknowledge and thank at least some of them. Of course, none of them is responsible for the final form. The mistakes are all my own.

The Nottingham Group for Social Justice gave of their time, energy and thoughtful good sense – and, anyway, I enjoyed all our meetings enormously. Thank you to Beryl Bennett, Max Biddulph, Carol Davies, Carolyn Goddard, June Hunter, David Martin, Syble Morgan, Prakash Ross, Jacky Smith, Nada Trikic and Sue Wallace. I am also grateful to Gwen Schaffer, who began with the group, but was unable to continue. Other people were helpful in that project, especially Mary Biddulph, Suzan Gokova and Kaye Haw, all of whom helped me to iron out issues of interviewing. Anne Seller and Judy Hughes helped at the first stages of formulation, in the course of a glorious week in the west of Scotland. Anne and I went on talking about the nature of a private or public space in an astonishing variety of settings, from the tea room at the National Gallery to the Peak District in early January. I learnt a lot too from my fellow organizers of symposia related to social justice at the British and European Educational Research Conferences in 1996: Rob McBride, Tony Sewell and Gaby Weiner. (Seville in late September was a particularly pleasant place in which to learn.) In the final stages, much later, very many thanks are due to Jacky Brine, John Coldron, Kaye Haw, Mary Hayes and Peter Bowbrick, who all managed to read it, thoughtfully, critically and most of all quickly, at a time when they were all extremely busy and hard pressed with other things. It all took rather longer than I had expected, and I was very grateful to my colleagues in the Faculty of Education at Nottingham Trent University, and to Pat Sikes, series editor, and Shona Mullen at Open University Press, for their understanding, advice, support and help.

Part I | Introduction and context

1 | Taking sides, getting change

Introduction

This is a book about using research for working towards justice, fairness and equity in education. It is about starting the process of educational research with a set of values that guide decisions about *what* is researched, and *how* and *why*. In other words, it is about taking sides and getting change in education through educational research. As Troyna and Carrington (1989: 208) point out, in their article 'Whose side are we on?, ethical dilemmas in research on "race" and education', commitment need not be 'a sentimental commitment to the "underdog".' They say: 'The researcher's pre-eminent commitment should not be to black or white youth, teachers or administrators, but to the fundamental principles of social justice, equality and participatory democracy.'

This book addresses questions of committed research. Does having a political or ethical position make the research biased and suspect from the start? Or, as I claim in this book, does acknowledging such a position improve the research? The book also addresses questions asked by those who want to do educational research for social justice. What special factors need to be taken into account by a researcher who is trying to do research for social justice? In practical terms, what sort of research techniques and methodologies are most appropriate? In answering these questions it also addresses two underlying, larger, questions. What is educational research for? How does that affect the process of educational research? Various possible answers are discussed: searching for truth; empowering others; empowering oneself and ourselves; giving or getting a voice; guiding and influencing policy change; engaging in political processes of change in education.

'Social justice' is a term which does not mean the same to everyone who uses it. The same is true of the term 'educational research'. I summarize my own view of social justice at the end of this chapter. However, it is not my intention to close these debates by imposing my own definition from the start, excluding consideration of alternatives. I take sides in the debate – and, indeed, I hope by this book to change some of the terms of it. At the same time, I try to acknowledge and work with the diversity of understandings, even though some of the differences are serious, even bitter. So as the book progresses – and especially in Chapters 5 and 6 – I take a particular position on what constitutes social justice and on the nature of educational research. I also propose some principles for doing educational research for social justice. I go on to use these principles to structure the discussions of practicalities of dealing with different stages of educational research in Part III. These are discussions, rather than definitive recommendations, because, as I shall explain, it is part of the logic of the set of principles that they are acted upon at the same time as knowing that they must always remain in question.

Writing and reading a book

A book is an act of communication shaped by the way it takes place in a particular context. The readers have to understand what the writer is saying, react to it, form judgements about it and possibly act on it. The writer has to imagine a probable set of readers, their reactions and judgements. This is particularly relevant in writing a book about justice in research. In writing such a book, I cannot avoid contradictions and dilemmas related to who gets to be writer and who gets to be audience for the book.

My being in a position to write the book at all has already involved negotiating a multiplicity of forms of power. This is a negotiation which has had to take into account my own personal, professional, social and political positionings – that is, how I am positioned in these terms by others, how I position myself and the way these two perspectives interrelate. Part of that positioning is reflected in the audience I take myself to be addressing when I write – and how I imagine that they (you) will react to it. Part of it is related to the global, historical, social context in which such a book comes to be written and published, bought and read.

In this section I introduce myself, discuss my imagined audience and briefly mention some relevant aspects of the historical context. For the reader, knowing something about the writer's identity and intentions helps in responding to the book. (Is she a school teacher? A student? Black? All three? And so forth.) For the writer, the imagined audience constrains how the book is constructed: which arguments and examples to use, and how much detail to include. (Are they scholastic academics? Or beginning teachers?) Lastly, the historical context in which we find ourselves affects the possible meanings of any argument. It is widely held that we are now living in conditions of globalization and migration, and are all dealing with the fast moving pace of change, which affects the meaning ascribed to justice.

Purposes and intentions: a personal journey

My own purposes and intentions in writing this book include, of course, the many personal pleasures and rewards of writing in this area of educational theory and practice. They also include the institutional pressures on academics to publish – and the institutional rewards of doing so. However, I focus not on these, but rather on the particular content and the way I express it here.

I have spent quite a lot of my professional life trying to improve social justice through educational research, and, conversely, educational research through social justice. However, there was a time, many years ago, when I thought I could look for educational improvement through research, without also considering the claims of social justice. Indeed, there was a time, even more years ago, when I thought I could detach my work from both practical and political concerns altogether, simply enjoying the pleasures of academic understanding. I have made a long journey since then, and it has taken that long journey for me to understand how little of the terrain I understood when I began. Then, when I got a better sense of how its underlying contours continue to influence academic and educational matters, I found I had to spend quite a lot of time looking for maps to help me find my way. I got some help from wrongly drawn maps, especially when their authors were prepared to amend them. I was less helped by people who were offering me maps meant to help me get to other places altogether – often to other kinds of research activity.

Having reached a place where I understand the terrain much better (or so it seems to me), I want to do two things. I want to draw the map even more clearly for myself, to make sure I get where I want to, and, at the same time, I want to make it available to others who might find it useful in walking their own paths.

When I started postgraduate research after a period of teaching, I was mainly interested in the philosophies of language and of emotion as they impinge on education. I wrote dissertations on these subjects. It was only as I came to the end of this period of writing that the significance of gender and class started to become apparent to me. My own class, race and gender position is relevant here. I am a white woman, born and partly brought up in colonial Africa. When I left at the age of ten, I had come to an imperfect understanding of social class as it manifested itself in England. At the same time, I was imbued with the way the white colonial world constructed the social sphere, with all its particular articulations of race, class and gender. An identity cannot be simply read off from a socio-economic position, as I have argued elsewhere (Griffiths, 1995a). It is probably relevant that I was born into a line of independently minded women on both my mother's and my father's side. It is probably also relevant that a high proportion of them, like the men they were married to, were teachers, clerics or public service administrators. It is not surprising that I have been drawn into trying to make sense of class, gender and race issues in an educational context.

My new-found interest in the significance of social categories, and gender in particular, led me into the then barely known field of feminist philosophy. I came to see the significance of there being no possibility of creating a 'god's eye view' on the world. A significant influence was that standpoint episte-mology and an epistemology of partial perspectives were being formulated at that time. Then, even more than now, such explorations were being car-ried out in the teeth of people firmly asserting there could be no such thing (see Chapter 4).

I have always been interested in *all* kinds of educational research, from philosophical to empirical. Indeed, I have always liked being in the kind of area in which the connections between the apparently theoretical or practi-cal, the apparently philosophical or empirical, can be built on and investi-gated. My work on emotions in the field of philosophy, together with my continuing interest in gender, led me to carry out a survey into the gendered aspects of the introduction of computers into primary schools. The survey was influenced by the work I had done on philosophy and emotion. (One of the theoretical articles I wrote at the time was called 'Strong feelings about computers'.) At the same time, my thinking about gender influenced and was influenced by both forms of research, philosophical and empirical. I had begun to see dimly how research and political positions were not mutually contaminating, but, rather, were inextricable, though I would not have phrased it like that then. (See Part II for more on this.) At the same time, I found that while I thought the results of the research should be significant for educational practice, actually making an impact on what was going on in schools was very difficult indeed. Even making any impact on the practice of the students on our courses was difficult (by this time I was lecturing in a university department of education), let alone affecting what was going on anywhere else. In retrospect, it was here that I began to develop my under-standing of *educational* research as research that improves the education of children and students (see Chapter 5).

Partly as a result of all this, I came to see that there is also the historical context to be taken into account. A significant aspect of this is the global context of Britain: a Western, English-speaking country, politically and geo-graphically at the edge of Europe, trying to reconstruct itself in conditions of rapid economic, political and demographic changes, which are often described as postcolonial and postmodern. In short, the context in which I am situated, and in which I act, is that of educational research in the West-ern, English-speaking world, particularly Britain, at the end of the twentieth century. However, it should not be thought that what goes on in other places is not relevant to the arguments of this book. I have regularly drawn on research from contexts other than my own immediate one.

The path I was treading was thronged with other people – not all going the same way. I was pushed and pulled by a number of others with whom I came into contact. At the same time, I was hearing the shouts and whispers of others treading similar paths – or refusing them and, indeed, sometimes issuing dire warnings that we were going in the wrong direction. We were warned that we might be running into all kinds of dangers. These shouts and whispers continue, and more and more people have joined in. Martyn Hammersley (1997: 141), who has issued several warnings over the years, says:

> The effects of what has been termed the 'crisis of representation', which increasingly afflicts the whole of humanities and social sciences . . . throw doubt on the capacity of research to produce knowledge, in the commonly accepted sense of that term.

He is referring here to the continuing and often raging debate about bias, objectivity, positivism and the production of useful knowledge. This debate is part of the context of this book – and equally this book is a contribution to that debate.

I am not contributing to a debate just for academic reasons. I am also trying to act politically: to influence the parameters of the debate in order to effect changes in educational practices. So I am trying to state the reasons for my approach persuasively because I believe it has the potential to contribute to the improvement of the education of all, and so to the improvement of the society in which we all live. To say this is to state a view of political rhetoric as persuasion rather than as propaganda. Integral to the approach is the importance of addressing the reasons why other people hold other positions, and engaging with them, rather than dismissing them as wrong-headed or as having ethically dubious motivations (as so often happens, even in apparently rational debates). Therefore, as well as drawing maps for my own use, and to help others, the book should provide some introductions to different schools of map drawing. I hope the result of this is to deepen and clarify discussions of epistemology and of power in the context of postmodern debates, and of methodologies of feminism and anti-racism, at the same time as showing how such abstract questions relate to the real, everyday, practical, mundane business of research. I cover the abstract questions of epistemology and of practical questions of technique, and, in both cases, provide some answers to accusations of bias or co-option which are likely to be levelled at researchers who get off the fence: 'You would say that, wouldn't you?' 'You've sold out and become one of them.'

Audience

Even to mention audience is to make a political statement. Writers who are not sharply focused on justice issues rarely comment on the question of audience. On the other hand, a recurring theme for writers interested in justice issues is the question of their imagined audience and how to address it. For instance, it is noticeable how often American black women writing justice-related theory feel the need to make their strategy explicit. bell hooks describes how she decided to leave footnotes out of her books in order to make them more friendly to the kind of working-class black communities in the United States in which she was brought up. She points out that she was warned that this decision would make her work less 'credible in academic circles' (hooks 1989: 81). In a similar vein, Patricia Hill Collins (1990: xii) says

> I was committed to making this book intellectually rigorous, well researched, and accessible to more than the select few fortunate enough to receive elite educations. I could not write a book about Black women's ideas that the vast majority of African-American women could not read and understand.

This is a political problem, because it is about the participation and exclusion of sectors of the community from the world of the writer.

A related political problem is to be found in much qualitative research. The difficulty lies in the differences between the perspectives, preferred language and, to some extent, the research agendas of teachers, academics and policy-makers. The problem lies in the significance of such differences if the research is to be accessible to those who took part in it. If research is to have an influence on practice, then such differences become even more significant. This is, again, a question of participation and exclusion from influence, though in this case there is more ambiguity about who holds the power over practice and policy.

The audience for a book such as this one is always going to be diverse. In particular, it will come from a variety of different positions in relation to powers in society at large. Within the UK, the context is one in which there is great variation among educational researchers with regard to levels of sophistication about doing research. Educational research is carried out by academics, senior teachers, classroom teachers, local education authority (LEA) officials and research consultants recruited by government or pressure groups. This pattern is likely to continue.

The audience is even more diverse than this. While some educational researchers will be working in the UK context, other researchers (including some working or studying in the UK) will come from a range of countries, including those which are not of the West. In this book I focus on the UK context, because I write in the belief that a critical appraisal of action is best undertaken from within it (Seller 1994; Griffiths 1995a). As I describe and reflect on my own context, I expect that this will enable people from other ones to understand and reflect on their own, since I can do the same with work from other contexts. For instance, I found Ladson-Billings's careful analysis of successful teaching for African-American students in the United States illuminating (Ladson-Billings 1994). I use her insights into her context to enable me to understand my own. However, neither she, nor I, can simply transport concepts and principles from one context to another. For I am also

acting on the belief that the links that unite different contexts are best understood by the people that inhabit them.[1]

To summarize: you, the readers, may work either in or out of the academy.
You may be students or professors. You may be classroom teachers working
with no research budget at all, or you may command the larger-scale
resources of government, local authorities or the European Union (EU). You
may come from contexts which are very different from those in Britain. It is
hoped that all of you could pick this book up and find something of value for
you. But, in particular, I want to be sure that those on the margins of research
– that is, precisely, those who are likely to be doing research for social justice
– are included as central, not marginal. My experience of researchers in social
justice is that I am likely to be addressing practising teachers, part-time
students and contract researchers, who may have a shortage of time, money
or institutional support, but who have a commitment to getting their research
right, and using it to make a difference. Those studying in academic institutions will need to be able to answer questions about how appropriate their
methodology is. Those researching in other workplaces will need to answer
questions from their funders and colleagues about bias and objectivity.

Historical context

All research, in its concern to make a contribution to knowledge, tends to
focus on innovation and originality. And educational research, in its concern
with making a difference to schools, tends to focus on the recent context of
educational practice. Given these tendencies, it is all the more important
to pay attention to the wider historical context, lest our understanding
becomes blinkered and parochial.

A history of educational research which is concerned with social justice in
Britain demonstrates that it is an approach which is neither new nor strange;
though the emphasis changes, as does the terminology. The movement
towards equality and equal opportunities can be said to have been going on
for centuries, constituting a significant strand (together with economic
activity and cultural development) in what Raymond Williams memorably
called 'the long revolution' (Williams 1985). While it is a continuous tradition, attention to social justice issues has gone in and out of academic and
political fashion, as has the approval of words such as 'equality', 'social justice', 'social emancipation' and 'social inclusion'. In Britain, in 1997, social
justice became a term which the government used with approval; this followed more than a decade in which it had been constructed as being danger-
ously opposed to economic efficiency (Ball 1997; quoted in Chapter 10).
Before that, in 1977, Denis Lawton was asserting that there was no essential
conflict between the 'two major themes' of educational development: economic efficiency and social justice (Lawton 1977: 1).

The continuity of a tradition of educational research for social justice can be traced in state policies and related government inquiries and reports. In Britain, in the first part of the twentieth century, the movement was focused on social class, and was expressed in the pushes towards meritocracy (for instance, in the adoption of the supposedly neutral 11+ examination) and towards egalitarian conceptions of education which would benefit children of all social classes (for instance, in the establishment of community schools). Lawton (1977) gives a historical overview of developments related to social class, describing the continuing, but at the same time halting, movement towards greater social justice in respect of social class. He traces a story which is one of increasing *formal* access to education for all classes; and which, at the same time, is subject to the continuing baleful influence of the nineteenth-century belief in 'two nations': the lower and upper orders. David Hamilton (1990), from a historical perspective less narrowly focused on social class than Lawton, tells a story of the double-edged progress of school-ing for all, in terms of its close connection with social transformations in gen-eral. More pessimistic than Lawton, Hamilton points out how acculturation, literacy and the division of labour provide the educational means of forming an elite. Still, as he also points out, the cultural possessions of the elite are sometimes extended to the excluded – or occasionally seized by them – lead-ing to the opportunity of their exerting some leverage on the direction of social change (Hamilton 1990: 36): 'People who had been taught through authorized texts simultaneously acquired tools which gave them access to politically contentious works like Thomas Paine's *Rights of Man* (1791) and Mary Wollstonecraft's *Vindication of the Right of Woman* (1792).'

Hamilton documents a history of struggle over the kind of society that is wanted, a struggle for social justice. He is careful not to present this as a movement describable as progress. Rather, he documents change and struggles for social justice which contribute to that change. The outcome of one such struggle, in Britain, was the creation of the welfare state, in which schooling was taken to be an important arm. The 1944 Education Act was drafted in a spirit of social idealism, and was 'intended to remove stigmas attached to "lower class education" . . . and set education in a framework of improved welfare and social justice' (Lawson and Silver 1973). Hamilton comments that 'Schooling attracted many teachers and educationists . . . who espoused a commitment to social justice and the equality of oppor-tunity' (Hamilton 1990: 79). Among these were educational researchers, intent on contributing through empirical knowledge and theoretical critique to the project of social justice through education.

There were numerous research reports in the area of social class examin-ing the effects of the welfare state, and of the 1944 Education Act. Floud and Halsey (1957) examined the effects of methods of selection on the social class of boys gaining the grammar school places which were the route to an academic education. Jackson and Marsden (1962) and Lacey (1970) used qualitative methods to explore the effects on working-class children of attending grammar schools. In another qualitative study based on interviews, Willis (1977) focused specifically on the reasons why working-class lads in a comprehensive school continued to demonstrate a rejection of educational opportunities by leaving school at the first opportunity and taking unskilled jobs. Lodge and Blackstone (1982) focused on the failure of educational policy in relation to equality, by examining the roles played by national and local government and various educational pressure groups.

In the 1970s and 1980s, the movement for social justice in terms of social class expanded into a movement for race and sex equality in education. Researchers were keen to contribute to this movement. To begin with, these studies were published by black and feminist presses. It took some time before mainstream publishers, including mainstream academic publishers, would support such research. Coard's (1971) study disclosing the over-representation of 'West Indian children' in British schools was an early and influential spur to research into racism in education. At about the same time, feminist research into the effects of sexism began to be published, largely in specialist feminist books and journals. It would be another decade before all this research came to the attention of a wider audience. The Rampton Report and the Swann Report came out in the early 1980s. Spender's (1982) book documenting a decade of research on girls in education was enormously influential. Indeed, from being a radical addition to social justice debates, by the beginning of the 1990s race and gender issues had nearly eclipsed social class as a focus for attention. Meanwhile, sexuality and disability were emerging as issues in equal opportunities alongside race and gender (Rieser and Mason 1992). However, by the early 1990s all these perspectives on social justice came under pressure because of what Kate Myers has described as a prevailing 'equiphobia' (Myers 1990). This pressure coincided with a greatly increased interest in the other of Lawton's 'main themes' of educational development: economic efficiency.

The movement I have described, invoking as it does Williams's 'long revolution', has overtones of the modernist march of progress. These overtones were not part of Hamilton's account, in spite of his evident commitment to justice and the struggle for justice. It is generally agreed that the march has changed its nature, if not actually been disbanded. There is now widespread discussion of what is variously referred to as postmodernism, postmodernity or late modernity. All these terms point to the effects of the development of new technologies, mass communications, globalization, widespread migration of peoples, transnational economies and an increased rate of change of social conditions. It has become clear that social justice is no longer a matter of liberation for one or other community or sector. Those communities and sectors are increasingly hard to identify at a time when political identities have become complex, fragmented and shifting. However, it has also become clear that the new conditions bring with them new formations of control and surveillance, provoking new modes of struggle for justice.

All these changes can be – and are – described in utopian or dystopian terms. The debate is symptomatic of uncertainty. In Britain, as in the rest of the world, changes in the governance and technologies of education require a radical rethinking of old practices. The powers of local authorities have given way to increasing centralization of power on the one hand, and, on the other, its drastic fragmentation. There has been increased emphasis on the new technologies of the 'information superhighway'. Productivity and performance have intensified the pace of work (Hargreaves 1994; Elliott 1996). At the same time, there is a change in the relationship between education, training and work. In the name of the creation of a more highly skilled and flexible workforce, there has been a shift in power and resources away from traditional providers of training and education. This has been combined with a move towards assessment and accreditation-led learning. The resulting unfamiliar, shifting, uncertain context of education is the background against which educational research needs to be carried out.

The scope of the book

Social justice

While I acknowledge and work with a diversity of understandings related to social justice, inevitably my own (evolving) understanding must structure how I articulate this diversity. At this stage, I give a brief explanation of what I mean by social justice by stating three principles. Later, in Chapter 6, I give a rationale for these principles, and then go on to give more detail of how they might be unfolded in relation to educational research, in the form of ten more detailed, more concrete, principles for action.

The first principle is that there is no one right answer. Establishing social justice is less about particular outcomes than about processes, including processes which may overturn themselves. A socially just state of affairs is one characterized by a continual checking and adjusting. It is not a static perfect system: utopia is not to be found. Gandhi is supposed to have said that 'Equality is not the end, it is the way.' The same applies to social justice.

The second principle is that each individual is valuable and recognized as an important valued part of the community as a whole. On the other hand, there is a recognition that no individual exists apart from her community – or, more accurately, communities, since she certainly belongs to more than one. Thus, the good of a community inevitably has implications for the good of the individual. Likewise, the good of the individual has implications for the good of her communities. To address two contrary fears about social justice issues: on the one hand, there is no thought that the interests of the individual are sacrificed to those of the community, although there may need to be a process of negotiation to discover how each can best be served. Equally, on the other hand, there is no thought that the interests of the individual override the interests of the community. Again, there may need to be a process of negotiation to get the maximum good for both.

The third principle is that just as we create ourselves in and against community, we create ourselves in and against sections of that community, as persons with gender, social class, race, sexuality and (dis)abilities. This principle draws attention to the importance of structural injustice, but in keeping with the second principle, also remains with individuals. Social justice is concerned both with individual empowerment and also with structural injustices; that is, with questions of power and resources available to individuals and to particular communities or sectors of those communities.

Qualitative research

Clearly, educational research for social justice is a huge area. I want to point out that it includes both quantitative and qualitative research. I make this clear in the next chapter, when I give some examples of 'research for social justice': I include research which is statistically based, for instance, and dependent on quantification. That said, in this book I focus on the part which can be described as 'qualitative' research. Much of what I say about 'research' may well pertain to both qualitative and quantitative research, but I never explicitly consider how far that is true.

Most people who have done some research – or used the results of research – have some feel for the meaning of the term 'qualitative'. But it is an inexact term, which has got caught up with all kinds of debates about the validity, ethics and usefulness of research. There is a further confusion, in that 'qualitative' can refer to a tradition of research or to kinds of data. So qualitative research can produce numbers but still be seen as 'qualitative' – just as quantitative research can draw on episodes of exploratory qualitative research in order to find categories to be quantified.

Unfortunately for anyone who is not already immersed in this debate, it has thrown up so much heat and dust that it is hard to tell what is being included as 'qualitative research', and why the term is significant as a boundary marker. There is a reason for all the commotion. Allegiances to particular forms of research, qualitative and quantitative, have political and ethical overtones, which generate heat. By now the debate also has a history, even mythology: this is dust which can obscure the issues as they apply in current contexts, but it is also dust which has permeated the issues and has to be recognized as changing their present nature.

The term 'qualitative' is one that gets its meaning in opposition to the term 'quantitative' – and vice versa. Historically, a tradition of self-styled qualitative research grew up in counterpoint to research which emphasized the methods of the earth sciences, particularly physics: an analytic search for simple categories, quantification, the use of mathematics, prediction, the search for laws and the accumulation of certain knowledge which is technically useful. The counterpoint took more than one form: sometimes appearing as triangulation for, sometimes as enrichment of, sometimes as an alternative to, quantitative work (Porter 1995). Either way, it developed much of its meaning by reference to what it is *not*: positivist, universal, statistical, predictive. This has been well described in a number of books and collections, usually critically (Bryman 1988; Dey 1993; Bryman and Burgess 1994; Denzin and Lincoln 1994). This way of understanding the issues has the advantage of a simple structure which can be grasped fairly easily. However, as I argue in later chapters, this simplicity is deceptive and ultimately unhelpful, because it obscures the real contours of the debates. In this book, I shall take it that qualitative research is research that uses at least some data that are not susceptible to numerical analysis.

The story continues

This chapter has been setting the scene. The next chapter continues that process. It considers some examples of research which could be claimed as research 'for social justice'. These examples will be used (with others) in the rest of the book to ground the abstract arguments.

The book is arranged in three parts. The first part is introductory and context setting. Parts II and III raise theoretical and practical considerations. Chapter 6 introduces a set of principles to guide educational research for social justice. These principles are crucial to both Parts II and III. Part II is more oriented to theoretical arguments underlying the principles and Part III is more oriented to the practical activities of research. However, I do not want to give the impression that theory precedes practice any more than practice precedes theory: I do not believe either is true. The book has been written on the assumption that theorizing is relevant to practical actions, and, conversely, practical actions are relevant to theorizing.

There is no need to read from start to finish, or even to read Part II before Part III. In writing this book, I have assumed that not everyone will read it straight through from start to finish. Indeed, people may only want to read single chapters. Or they may want to come back to particular sections at a later stage, when their memory of the details of other sections has faded. So I have included brief summaries and cross-references all the way through. Anyone reading the book in one go, from start to finish, should skip them! There are also short introductory sections before Parts II and III to help busy, hard-pressed readers to find their way through the book in the order that best suits them.

Note

1 To take another example, Freire's (1972) discussion of the liberating power of education remains influential in a range of countries and contexts – though it was written in the context of Brazil in the 1960s.

2 | Research for social justice? Some examples

People new to this kind of research might assume that there is something called social justice, which is simply identified as the object of research; they might therefore assume that it is something which could be sharply defined, even if, so far, they have only a hazy idea of it. This is far from the case.

This chapter summarizes some examples of educational research and discusses why – and how far – each of them counts as research for social justice. Four of these examples are accounts of research by other people and the fifth is research which I carried out, in collaboration with others, into the nature of social justice in education. The purpose of the description is to develop a preliminary understanding of the kinds of things that I am referring to in this book as 'social justice'. They serve as a kind of ostensive definition, a way of delineating an area by pointing at it. The discussion points forward to arguments later in the book, in which I draw lines of demarcation around 'research for social justice'. So one purpose of the discussion is to indicate how I will be developing a way of focusing down from the overall area, to see the complexities of the object in the viewfinder. My discussion suggests that, far from being simple, the object is both complex and shifting.

A research review on ethnic minority pupils

David Gillborn and Caroline Gipps (1996) *Recent Research on the Achievements of Ethnic Minority Pupils*. London: HMSO (Ofsted). This is a review of research into race and achievement in Britain. It was commissioned because of widespread disquiet about the educational performance of ethnic minorities in relation to examination results, behaviour and exclusion figures. It is, therefore, directly concerned with social – racial – justice in educational settings. The report briefly summarizes the main findings of relevant research and includes explanations about how to weigh the evidence and about the meanings of some of the key terms.

In late 1996, an eagerly awaited report came out, summarizing educational research into race and achievement. Commissioned by Ofsted, it follows the format of such government documents, rather than the format of most academic educational research. In the first section, it reviews research results in the area of the achievement of ethnic minority pupils at different points in their educational careers. However, it does not stop there. In the other three sections, research into the context of such achievement is reviewed: into educational progress and school effectiveness; into day-to-day experiences of teachers and pupils; and into recent trends in post-compulsory education.

I have chosen to include this document as an example of research for social justice for several reasons. In the first place, research on ethnic minority achievements is always a good candidate for the description 'research for social justice', and, indeed, most of the research reviewed in the document would fit such a label. However, I also want to draw attention to the document as a whole, because I would claim that it is more than a simple review of research; rather, it is, in itself, the result of a small piece of research activity, carried out with the intention of increasing knowledge and promoting better practice in education with regard to ethnic minority pupils. It is no accident that the authors are extremely experienced, highly respected researchers. Such a review is not a mechanical task carried out by doing a bibliographic search of keywords using one of the abstracting services (whether electronic or print-based). The document is significant just because experienced researchers, already working in the field, have selected which bits of research appear, in what order and with appropriate remarks about how much weight can be placed on various sources of evidence. It is worth noting the wide range of kinds of research which are included for review: they include qualitative and quantitative approaches in work carried out by LEAs, Ofsted, pressure groups and academic institutions. They also include more theoretically based research. For instance, introductions to the sections include discussions of some of the conceptual difficulties in terms like 'under-achievement'.

Any problems in describing this piece of work as 'research for social justice' arise from a way of describing the research differently from looking at the content of the research findings. This review was commissioned by Ofsted, a government body. It was put out to tender, and the bid that was accepted came from the London Institute of Education, one of the most prestigious and high-status educational research institutions in the country. In other words, this is research that has been carried out at the behest of the government, by researchers in a powerful, London-based, academic institution, reviewing research which is already shaped by its entanglement with – indeed, dependence on – the institutions of government and higher education. On the one hand, such research is clearly very well placed to inform policy. On the other hand, it reflects the perspectives of institutions which are, according to much social justice research, themselves likely to be part of the problem. Of course, this is not enough in itself to cast serious doubt on the document, though it should give pause for thought. The thought is worth pursuing! Only when critical attention is paid to power relations of all kinds can their complexity be taken into account in judging research. For instance, it is worth noticing that the review was carried out by two individuals who have been exercising their agency to look for spaces in the structures they inhabit; and have demonstrated that they are committed to doing so by the kinds of research they have produced – and continue to produce – during their careers. Finally, each of those individuals is enmeshed in the power relations that run through our society: gender, race, sexuality, class, age, region, religion – including how all of these are constructed in relation to countries outside Britain/Europe.

The content of the review – the achievement of ethnic minority pupils – makes it a good candidate for description as 'research for social justice'. But I am arguing that this is only a beginning. Questions such as 'Carried out by whom?' 'Where?' 'Who paid?' and 'For what purpose?' are all just as relevant as the more obvious questions like 'What was it about?' These questions are addressed to researchers at an institutional level and also at an individual level. Other examples point up these questions, in some cases even more sharply.

Questions of feminist and anti-racist approaches

Mehreen Mirza (1995) Some ethical dilemmas in field work: feminist and antiracist methodologies. In M. Griffiths and B. Troyna (eds) *Antiracism, Culture and Social Justice in Education.* Stoke-on-Trent: Trentham. Mehreen Mirza, herself a British South Asian woman, examines the ethical dilemmas of researching gender/race issues. Drawing on evidence from her own research into the educational experiences of South Asian women and girls in the North West of England, she questions standard feminist and anti-racist approaches to resolving ethical and practical dilemmas of research. It is a piece of research into research methodology, and is explicitly commenting on the ways in which 'research as praxis' can advance social justice in relation to providing a means through which her research subjects could voice their opinions and present their experiences without becoming pathologized or stereotyped by more powerful people.

The second example of educational research that could be characterized as 'for social justice' is, in effect, a reflective, second-order research project into a first-order research project. Both could be described as 'for social justice'. Mehreen Mirza's article discusses some dilemmas facing her, as a researcher, in using feminist and anti-racist methodologies. The example in the previous section (Gillborn and Gipps's review of research into the achievements of ethnic minority pupils) was carried out by well known, white researchers in a prestigious institution. Like everyone else, of course, they had to begin their careers as unknown. Mirza's article is written by someone at the beginning of her career. Indeed, it was published in the form it was partly because Mirza *was* a new researcher. The article appears in a collection by myself and Barry Troyna. As we stated in the Introduction, one of the criteria for inclusion in the collection was that we 'wanted to include researchers relatively new on the scene' (Griffiths and Troyna 1995: xvi). Another significant criterion was the importance of including 'researchers who vary in their own subject position, for instance in relation to "race" and gender' (*ibid.*).

Mirza's research project could be said to be 'for social justice' in both its content and its method. The aim of the research was 'to gain an insight of the experiences of South Asian girls' and women's experiences of education in "non-traditional" areas' of the curriculum (Mirza 1995: 164), using a qualitative research methodology in order to allow them to raise their own issues and concerns. However, Mirza's claim to be doing research for social justice is much stronger than this, as she explains in her reflective research into related methodological issues. She argues that research is inherently political, partly because the academy has been dominated by the political values and commitments of white, middle-class and/or male researchers. The article is fascinating for the way she systematically investigates her own research practice in trying to carry out the principles of feminist and anti-racist research in the ways usually recommended in the literature – when she, as a South Asian woman, is both an insider and an outsider of the community being researched.

Mirza, like Gillborn and Gipps, works for an institution of higher education, and, like them, she was contracted to do the research and so had only limited autonomy in designing it. On the other hand, unlike with them, her institution is not one of the most prestigious in the country, and unlike them, she was not employed by an agency of the central government with a strong influence on policy. Further, she, like everyone, is enmeshed in the power relations that run through our society: gender, race, sexuality, class and the rest. She argues that her particular position in these structures gives her an epistemological advantage. This is not an essentialist argument, however. That is, it is not an argument that thinks South Asian women have some common, essential nature.[1] On the contrary, she regards an outcome of her research, precisely, as the overcoming of 'essentialist perspectives of South Asian womanhood' (Mirza 1995, 180). Like Gillborn and Gipps, Mirza is exercising her agency to look for spaces in the structures she inhabits.

The organization of schools

Stephen Ball (1987) *The Micro-politics of the School: towards a Theory of School Organization*. London: Routledge. This well known book proposes a theory of school organization based on two kinds of data: case studies and interviews. Stephen Ball provides a schema for the analysis of school organization, in order to provide an understanding of the micro-politics of school life: in relation to change, leadership, headship, careers, resources and relationships, in the context of the politics of age, gender and the macro-political climate. The theoretical framework depends on categories central to social justice: power, participation and their interaction with social structures of age and gender.

Research into organizations – or into educational management – is not, routinely, described as 'for social justice', in the way that research into the educational effects of gender, class or ethnicity is. However, this is, in my view, to regard the matter too narrowly. Educational research for social justice can look very much like any other kind of educational research with regard to the arena in which the research is carried out. Whether researchers are ostensibly researching management or curriculum, achievement or primary practice, education for work or literacy, there is a possibility that this research is also describable as 'for social justice'. On the face of it, research related to organizational theory (and educational management) could be thought of as one of the less promising areas, since it has a history of being theorized to reflect the interests and needs of managers (Ball 1987: 5). One of the most well known and influential pieces of research shows that this need not be the case. Stephen Ball's *The Micro-politics of the School* could be read as a contribution to the theory of school organization and as a project to ground the analysis in detailed, qualitative, ethnographic data, rather than in ideology (Ball 1987: 5–7). Indeed, it is often read just in this way. A closer look reveals the underlying concern with social justice. In presenting the theoretical framework as taking account of 'control' as well as of 'authority', and of 'conflict' as well as of 'consensus', he remarks on the importance of 'examining developments which are related to the achievement of more equal, more just, as well as more effective education' (*ibid.*: 3). It should not be surprising, then, that as well as chapters which examine leadership and headship, there are chapters explicitly concerned with age and gender issues. The book ends by quoting, with approval, from Aronowitz and Giroux, on the way struggle and contestation allows for the development of critical thinking and civic courage, and goes on:

Is the form of organizational life presented here the only possible form for funding schools? The answer must be 'no', and as I see it the alternative lies in the direction of *school democracy*. But that, as they say, is another story.

(Ball 1987: 280, italics in original)

In a reflection on the process of writing *The Micro-politics of the School*, Ball explains how it had its origin in frustrations he felt as a teacher and researcher in the University of Sussex, when trying to teach a course on 'the school as an organization' (Ball 1991). He thus positions himself, institutionally, in relation to schools and universities. He has positioned himself, implicitly, in relation to the power relations inherent in dealings between these different institutions. He does not do this explicitly. Although his work is, precisely, concerned with such power relations, he does not, in fact, reflect on them in relation to his own research. However, as his own subsequent work would indicate, the various positionings to which he is subject, and which he takes up, are relevant to the kind of research he can do (e.g. Ball 1990, 1991). In the course of those reflections, he also explains something of the personal processes of ethnography. However, he does not investigate the implications for his work of his own race, gender or social class. There is a contrast here with Mirza's reflections on her own research, where she argues that all these factors are of epistemological and methodological significance in terms of the kind of equality and justice which frame his research. It is worth pointing out that Ball's research is much older than any of the other pieces of research I have used in this chapter. In his later work, he goes further towards reflecting on his own positioning in relation to that of his research subjects (e.g. Ball 1997).

Action research, the exercise of power and collective political action

Melanie Walker (1995) Context, critique and change: doing action research in South Africa, *Educational Action Research*, 3(1), 9–27.
·The article presents an argument about the value of action research projects in South African settings, and about what can be learnt from them which is of general use for action researchers internationally. Three case studies are briefly presented and then discussed in relation to an autobiographically based discussion of some action research carried out by herself, researching her own practice as a white teacher educator of african[2] teachers. The point of the article is to suggest ways in which individual action research projects can contribute to collective political action for a social transformation of any society whose institutions are shaped by gender, race and class.

In her article, Melanie Walker reflects on action research through a discussion of her research into her own practice as facilitator of teachers'

development through curriculum changes (Walker 1995: 19). She was working in 'a historically black university struggling to embed a research ethos
and culture, and to throw off its apartheid origins as a "bush" college' (*ibid*.:
9). Like Mirza's article, this one is an example of reflective second-order
research on a research project. Like Ball's work, Walker's is an example of a
piece of research in which the content is apparently not something describable as 'social justice': that is, professional development and social change.
In her discussion of the research, Walker makes it clear that justice issues
were, in fact, central to the initial approach and to her subsequent reflections.

The purpose of action research is, always and explicitly, to improve practice. In this case, the practice in question is Walker's own. However, since her
professional role was 'facilitator of teachers' development', the aim of
improving her own practice was dependent on the aim of improving the
teachers' development. As I have described this so far, the action research
programme is neutral with respect to justice. Nothing has been said which
indicates an ethical position on what would count as teachers' development.
However, as Walker makes clear, she is similar to Ball, in that the direction
of her research and so her judgement of its success were underpinned by a
concern for social justice. From the start, she was concerned to know how
the teachers viewed the institutions that marginalized and excluded them. As
the research went on, this preoccupation with social justice issues led her to
investigate how that concern was expressed (*ibid*.: 20): 'The oppressive
effects of my own emancipatory wishes also need re-exploration in the way
I accounted for power relations between myself and teachers.' These power
relations are a complex interaction of racism, sexism, social class and academic roles. As a result, by the end of the research she was formulating the
social justice implications of facilitating teacher development in terms of
exercising 'one's own power in ways which enable others also to exercise
power' (*ibid*.: 21). She also raises the question of how to get 'from personal
development to collective political action', a question which she continues
to pursue in later work (e.g. Walker 1996a) in terms of developing a collective politics based on complex rather than simple ideas, and in a language of
practical hope founded on relatively small-scale and multiple struggles
rather than on grand or absolute claims about what constitutes emancipatory action.

An example of using the principles in a project about social justice in schools

Morwenna Griffiths and the Nottingham Group for Social Justice,
'Social justice in education: a theoretical framework for effective
practice'. This was a year's project funded through the ESRC[3] in the

academic year of 1995/6. I describe this piece of research from the inside, as one of the researchers, rather than from a published book or article. The intention of the project was, as its title suggests, to develop a theoretical framework which would be useful for practitioners – teachers and advisors – in improving social justice in schools. The research was run collaboratively and resulted in a set of twelve principles for senior management teams wanting to improve social justice in their schools.

The last example I discuss is research in which I was personally involved. This was a project about social justice in education, and I have used its results to structure this book. The aim of the research was to study the concept of social justice in the context of education, and to investigate how to implement it effectively in schools. The account of the research serves a double purpose in this book: as an example of research 'for social justice', with the same kinds of question marks over it as all other such pieces of research; and as further background explanation for some of the discussions of social justice. Therefore, I describe it in more detail than the other pieces of research in this chapter.

The project used, and further developed, an innovative methodology, which was influenced by the traditions of action research (reflective practice) and philosophy, and which was strongly influenced by a feminist, social justice perspective. It was thus extremely reflexive, since the core concepts influencing the methodology were themselves under investigation, and were developed as a result of carrying out the project. The logic here is not circular but iterative. The point was to spiral from theoretical considerations and abstractions to practicalities; and, further, from one set of theoretical views to another, from one set of practicalities to another. Dewey has had a great influence on modern understanding of action research, and, moreover, was a philosopher with a strong interest in social justice. His remarks on methodology remain relevant. Dewey (1916: 328) usefully described part of this process:

> Nevertheless we never get wholly beyond the trial and error situation. Our most elaborate and rationally consistent thought has to be tried in the world and thereby tried out. And since it can never take into account all the connections, it can never cover with perfect accuracy all the consequences. Yet a thoughtful survey of conditions is so careful, and the guessing at results so controlled, that we have a right to mark off the reflective experience from the grosser trial and error forms of action.

Elsewhere he says (*ibid.*: 150–1):

> Where a system becomes influential, its connection with a conflict of interests calling for some program of social adjustment may always be

discovered. At this point the intimate connection between philosophy and education appears. In fact, education offers a vantage ground from which to penetrate to the human, as distinct from the technical significance of philosophic discussions.

I was funded for a year to carry out this research, in collaboration with a number of people who work in schools. I chose to work with a team of twelve co-researchers who are deputy heads or members of various government-funded educational support services.[4] Deputy heads are uniquely placed to combine perspectives of classroom teachers and of senior management. They are senior managers, participating in most of the decisions of the head and the governors. They are also usually class teachers themselves, and closer to the everyday concerns of teachers than heads can be. Thus, they are particularly well placed to see the full complexity of the results of a number of centralized educational decisions – and they have to respond to them. Members of educational support services bring another perspective. They are in the business of negotiating directly with teachers and senior managers to influence practice in schools.

I was careful to ensure that the group included a variety of perspectives. This does not mean that they *represented* a variety of perspectives. They included people working in primary[5] and secondary schools; in the inner cities and in rural areas; in racially mixed and in predominantly white schools. They also included men and women; black and white; migrant, British born and first generation British; gay and straight. Between us, we came from a number of concrete contexts, in which the various constituencies mentioned above played a part in the kinds of perspectives we held.[6] However, none of us spoke on behalf of, or as a representative of, any particular group, and equally, almost nobody was one of a kind among the above categories. There were two exceptions. Special educational needs and sexuality are often overlooked as issues of social justice, so I especially included (a) someone from an educational psychology service and (b) a class teacher who also works as a consultant in educational issues related to gay, lesbian and bisexual young people. While these two people were aware of the reasons I wanted them in the group, they too spoke as themselves and not as representative of any wider group.

A central feature of the method was the intention of developing a sustained dialogue in spite of having chosen to work with some of the busiest people I know. It takes time to engage with others: to try and see their points of view; to work out areas of agreement and disagreement; and to discuss them. Thus, the numbers had to be limited. Even with a relatively small number of people, sustained dialogue is particularly difficult if it has to be fitted into already overcrowded professional lives, as was the case for my colleagues on the team. The project had to be designed to keep meetings as few, short and focused as possible for them – time was less of a problem for me because of my privileged position as directly funded to work on the project. I was aware that at the first of the focused meetings I would have already developed some views on the issues. I wanted to know what the other participants thought before I influenced them with my relatively explicitly worked out and already articulated views. I also chose to work with people who were already personally known to me in a professional context, so that time would not be spent negotiating social relationships.

With all these constraints in mind, I started by interviewing each person: listening rather than arguing. This first interview was, in effect, indistinguishable from an interview in standard educational research practice, used to collect data from research subjects. The interviews usually lasted for about an hour, using five semi-structured, open questions. I introduced the topic, by explaining that I took social justice to be a broad concept, and I went over the purposes of the project again. I also agreed the level of confidentiality for the interview. The questions covered the following areas:

1 How an interest in the issues developed.
2 How the issue has changed in schools since the ERA.
3 Critical incidents related to the issues.
4 What a 'good school' would be.
5 How schools should fit into society as a whole.

I tried not to react in a way which betrayed my own evaluations of what they said, but I already knew at the start that I could be only partly successful in this, because I knew the participants previously in professional contexts in which my own views had been expressed.

Each talk was then transcribed and sent to the participant. At this stage, I included my comments on it. For each one, I picked out what they had said. I used ten headings, in three sections. The first section picked out their own experiences relating to social justice and getting change in schools. The second section picked out what they had to say, if anything, about a number of concepts which were emerging from my reading or from the interviews as significant in constructing a framework. Under each heading I summarized what I thought had been said, and I also commented on where I had agreed, disagreed, had reservations or concerns, or was puzzled. Some of the group members found time to respond to my comments in writing. We then met three times as a whole group to discuss the progress of the project, the developing framework and the best direction in which to direct our efforts for practical change. These meetings were supplemented by individuals meeting each other or telephoning and carrying on discussions informally. I acted as minute taker between the group meetings, as well as keeping in touch informally. All this resulted in some adjustments to the framework and to a focusing and change of how the project will be taken forward. A lot of this discussion revolved around what would be appropriate language and which discourse to use if change is to be brought about.[7]

At the end of the year we came up with a set of principles (see Appendix). These were not intended to be any kind of universal answer to the question of what social justice in education might be – or how to get it. Rather, they were a kind of policy document for the particular contexts in which the participants worked, and which we supposed might be useful for similar ones. The purpose of producing such a document was to get change in the direction of improving social justice in schools. As is the nature of policy documents, it was marked by compromise rather than consensus – the kind of compromise where agreement goes as far as the document, but not necessarily further. To use Cynthia Cockburn's useful analysis, it is a document that is restricted to a short agenda, and there is no reason to suppose it might extend to a longer agenda (Cockburn 1989). At the same time as contributing to a collective endeavour, members of the group have used the project for their own purposes, as it was intended we should. I myself have made use of the project to theorize social justice – in this book, for instance.

My research project – our research project – is like Mirza's: not only its content but also its method is recognizably 'for social justice'. However, unlike her, I had designed the research, and therefore have a different responsibility in relation to its overall design and evaluation. As with Ball and Walker, both the direction of the research and my judgement of its success (in so far as I judge it to be successful, now or in the future) are underpinned by my concern for social justice. Thus, I recognize, explicitly now, as I did at meetings of the group, that however much I set it up as 'collaborative', involving 'co-researchers', it remained, in fact, mine more than theirs. I set up the methodology, chose the participants and decided the direction of investigation. I tried to set this up so that the group could change some or all of these, but, inevitably, the cards were stacked from the start. Anyway, change could only occur within the parameters of the funding, and within the parameters of the demands of the ESRC, which was the funder. The group was far more concerned than the ESRC would have been to do things, however small, in their own professional contexts. The ESRC, on the other hand, wanted evidence of more widespread impact, including theoretical advances. This stacking of the cards towards a certain kind of power nexus is reminiscent of Gillborn and Gipps's research. An intention to research for and through social justice is not enough to ensure that either the results or the methods fully meet the intention. However, as I shall argue later, criticisms need not be devastating, and judgements are more complex than a 'tick' or a 'cross'. This applies to me – to us – as it does to the rest of the pieces of research that I have discussed. Utopia is not around the corner, and research stories are always of a variety of failures as well as a range of successes.

Some categories

There is clearly a considerable variation in the pieces of research I have chosen as examples of research for social justice. They fall into three categories, which are not mutually exclusive. Most research for social justice would fall into two or even all three of them. The first two are as follows.

1 Research that is focused directly on justice issues. In the examples these are 'race' and South Asian women, but I could also have chosen a number of pieces of research into social class, special educational needs, gender and/or sexuality.
2 Research with a framework that depended on the researcher's orientation to justice issues but that is 'about' something else. In my examples from Ball and Walker, the research was 'about' school organization and teacher development.

This distinction is always significant. In any work to do with social justice, there is always a question of how far the issues should be treated directly and as a discrete topic, and how far they should be integrated into other topics. For instance, *The Runnymede Bulletin*, commenting on the decision by Ofsted to remove equal opportunities from the Framework[8] as a discrete topic, said the following:

> The Runnymede Trust was one of the bodies which regretted the intention to remove equal opportunities as a discrete topic. However, we readily acknowledge that, in education as in other fields of social policy, there are sound reasons for integrating equality issues with other topics and concerns rather than treating them separately.
>
> (No. 288, September 1995)

The third category is particularly important for this book, because it is about the methods of research and the reasons for choosing them.

3 Research in which the methodology or epistemology of the research is itself a reason for claiming it to be research for social justice.

It is claimed by some researchers that their epistemological positions and/or methodological approaches are themselves socially just. In the examples, this claim is made by Mirza on behalf of feminist, anti-racist perspectives. It is made by Ball on behalf of conflict theory in sociology, and of research which articulates the views and perspectives of teachers (Ball 1987: 3). It is made by Walker on behalf of a particular approach to action research: in which attention is paid 'to individual performance, to local struggles, and to praxis as committed, self-aware social action' (Walker 1996: 419).

The distinctions I am drawing in order to form these categories cut across the division into quantitative and qualitative research. I want to re-emphasize that research for social justice is not the prerogative of just one of these. How-ever, in the rest of the book I will look only at qualitative research. No doubt much of what I say, especially in Part II, could also apply to quantitative research, but I do not consider how far this might be so.

This third category will be examined in the course of this book. In the end I will be proposing a version of my own. However in its simple forms, it needs to be treated with caution. In particular, there are three questions which need to be raised. *First*, is the claim a call for purity? In other words, is it the claim that research for social justice can properly be carried out by one particular method only, and with only one particular epistemological stance? I will argue against such purity in Part II, especially in Chapters 5 and 6, and then again in Part III. *Second*, what is to be said about the iden-tity of researchers? How epistemologically significant are their sex, race or sexuality – or their identities as teachers, managers, policy-makers or edu-cational researchers? This will also be addressed in Part II. *Third*, what is the place of a political strategy for justice in the choice of particular approaches, especially given the practical and political constraints on research design and dissemination? Part III addresses this third set of questions about the more immediate and practical decisions to be made while doing research for social justice.

Notes

1 'Essentialism' is a term which is used to indicate an opposition to social construc-tion theories of various kinds. So an essentialist view of human beings, women or South Asian women would be one which explained their psychological character-istics in terms of something intrinsic to being, respectively, human, female or South Asian female. Non-essentialist explanations, in contrast, point to social context, language etc. This issue is a variant of the so-called 'nature–nurture' debate.

2 Melanie Walker uses lower case 'to signal that "african" is an indicator of an apartheid construction of a social or "racial" group' (1995: 25).

3 The research was funded by the ESRC under its Senior Research Fellowship scheme.

4 During the year the project was funded, two of them moved jobs: one deputy became a head, while another took early retirement. Since then, several more changes have occurred: one has moved into higher education, another into a differ-ent advisory role and a third out of education altogether.

5 I have included nursery under primary.

6 There is theoretical background to this terminology. I use the discussion of 'con-crete others' in Benhabib (1992) and their significance in challenging a politics built on the generalized Other. I discuss this further in Griffiths (1995a).

7 For some more detail of the process of adjustment, see Griffiths (1998b).

8 Ofsted is familiar to readers in Britain as the government body responsible for inspecting schools. It publishes a Framework which determines the form and focus of school inspections.

Part II | Theoretical frameworks for practical purposes

Introduction to Part II

This chapter marks the beginning of Part II of this book. Readers may want to continue here, reading this Part before they read Part III. But they should pause before they do so. Everything depends on the reader's needs and interests, and they need to consider these before deciding in what order to read the book. It is in the order it is for reasons of logic, not because this is necessarily the best way to read it. I wanted to explain how I arrived at the principles on which the discussions in Part III are based, before I discussed their use. However, readers might well want to take the principles as given and go straight to Part III.

As I said in Chapter 1, it is my view that the theoretical abstractions and the practical realities of research are so interrelated that each has to be understood alongside and in connection with the other (rather than either being prior to the other). It is for this reason that I have written this book to be read in an order that suits individual readers, knowing that they may well want to dip in and out of different chapters.

There could be several reasons for readers wanting to begin with Part II. Perhaps they have done quite a lot of research already and are looking for theoretical underpinnings to practical choices they have made. Or they are looking for challenges to the ideas they have developed already. Or perhaps they came to research precisely because they find abstract theory mind-stretching and intellectually satisfying. Perhaps they have reached that stage in an accredited research degree when they have to grapple with questions of methodology and epistemology, and they find that there is very little that directly addresses general questions related to social justice in educational research.

The language of Part II is suited to dense and difficult theorizing. I say something about so-called 'jargon' and its uses in Chapter 3. But before reading any of the chapters, readers need to be aware that these chapters are heavy, dense and difficult and they are like this because the issues they raise are themselves complex and the subject of much unavoidable debate, both inside and outside communities of educational research. (However, readers who already have a knowledge of these areas of debate may find these the easiest chapters.)

Principles on which to base decisions and choices about research are developed in Part II. In this part of the book I survey arguments and then marshal them to develop some principles of educational research for social justice. These are theoretically based but practically oriented. A summary of the principles can be found in the Introduction to Part III. The full version appears in Chapter 6, together with an explanation of how they relate to the three working principles outlined in Chapter 1. I summarize these three working principles briefly here, for ease of reference:

1 Social justice is at least as much about processes as it is about finding lasting solutions.
2 Individuals exist in communities and so the good for one has implications for the good of the other. Neither overrides the other.
3 Social justice is concerned to right both individual disempowerment and structural injustices of gender, social class, race, sexuality and disability.

It is with this general position in mind that Part II is structured. Chapter 3 looks at what it is to do research for the good of human beings. Chapters 4 and 5 discuss this further, in relation to the possibilities of gaining useful knowledge. Chapter 4 considers how the issues of fact, value, power and knowledge appear in relation to research for social justice. Chapter 5 addresses questions of uncertainty in relation to both values and knowledge. In Chapter 6, all these arguments are brought together to develop the principles of research for social justice which structure Part III.

3 | Truths and methods

Epistemology and methodology: the use of technical terms

The first two chapters referred to positionings related to power relations and to methodology. They also referred to the epistemological questions which underpin both these issues. This chapter explores all these issues further and discusses their significance for research to do with people, especially educational research for social justice. It is, of course, possible to do some educational research without paying explicit attention to power or epistemology, or even to methodology. It is still possible to proceed with educational research without even using such words. However, as I explain in this chapter, any piece of research, however small, cannot help but have an epistemology. It is also always implicated in power relations. And these factors always influence the methodology, even in those cases where they are not explicitly mentioned. Further, many of the bitter arguments about the significance of research findings are founded in fundamental disagreements about knowledge and how to get it: these are, precisely, disagreements about epistemology and methodology. The discussion of the five examples of 'research for social justice' in Chapter 2 showed how these issues, especially power relations and methodology, are inextricably part of the judgement of the worth of the research, especially in relation to social justice.

'Epistemology' and 'methodology' are technical terms, rather than part of the everyday language of most people working in educational contexts. However, I have chosen to use the technical terms, knowing that I risk being off-putting to some people who just want to get on with their research rather than deal with what they see as jargon. I have found that 'too much jargon!' is the reaction of many who want to do educational research, and who turn to academics for support. Of course, it is well known that what sounds like 'jargon' may just be the words specific to an area of work. Teachers and advisors have their own versions: their professional talk often sounds like jargon to outsiders.

But the difficulty of understanding another group's professional language is not the whole story in this case. There is another factor underlying the reaction of self-described practical people to the language of academics. The language of academics is understood to be part of the conversational style of a relatively powerful group of people which can be used to exclude others, and to put them at a disadvantage. In order to discuss this reaction – and what to do about it – I make use of Donald Schön's famous metaphor of the swamps of practice contrasted with the high ground of theory (Schön 1983). This is a rich metaphor, which includes in its imagery a hierarchy between theory and practice, thinking and doing, a hierarchy which is pervasive in Western thinking. Whether such a hierarchy should or even does exist is another matter. The metaphor is rich because, while it acknowledges how such a separation and hierarchy is part of the present connotations of the terms, it also enables us to rethink and recast it. I shall use this metaphor in this section, in order to do just that.

There are those of us who love theories and theorizing, who are willing to climb their heights, enjoying the exercise of grasping strange words and using them to reach new peaks of understanding. There are quite a lot of us, but, at least in the world of education, we are in a minority. Teachers, advisors and policy-makers have pressing practical problems to solve. They all have implicit theories about their problems and reflect on them continuously, but such reflections are rarely couched in the language of high theory which is habitually used by those who are less practically engaged in the educational issues they address. Many theorists, like myself, enjoy theory and theorizing for its own sake, as well as for its practical results. We stand accused by teachers and policy-makers of mystifying the important questions that need to be answered. It should be possible, it is said, to learn more about practical issues like the educational achievement of ethnic minorities, or the organization of schools, without being put off by the unnecessarily complicated terminology habitually used by researchers in universities.

I have a certain sympathy with this point of view. There is no doubt that language can be made unnecessarily complicated, and that its effect can be to exclude and puzzle the very people that it is supposedly meant to help and support. Worse, it can be used by those at home with the language of theory to embarrass those who are not, and make them feel ignorant, stupid or otherwise inferior.

So why do I persist in using terms like 'epistemology' and 'methodology'? Partly, I do so just because I would like to subvert and challenge the idea that 'high' knowledge is only for some people and 'low' knowledge is for the others. I would also like to subvert and challenge the idea that one set of them is superior. We need to acknowledge the uses of both kinds of knowledge for everyone. In metaphorical terms, I am drawing attention to the richness and fertility of the soft, low ground where we all live, while also acknowledging the appeal of the hard, high and barren peaks, and the beautiful views we get from them of the country as a whole. Further, and perhaps more importantly, I am drawing attention to the way in which the two kinds of knowing are inextricably related, dependent on each other, mutually influential and difficult to disentangle. Here the metaphor begins to break down, for the very good reason that it depends on untenable assumptions about differences between knowledge and skills; intellectual and non-intellectual work; theory and practice. I say more about this metaphor and the inextricable, mutual dependence of theorizing and practical context in an article (Griffiths 1998a) which draws on an earlier one, in which I discussed the mindfulness of skill and the implications of reasoning itself being a practical activity (Griffiths 1987).

In the case of theorizing about knowledge and how to get it, terms like epistemology and methodology are helpful. Using the terms helps in accessing relevant arguments, and also in accessing a language in which to discuss important differences about what is known or knowable. The questions are not simple or closed. Rather, there are deep and complex issues at stake, which need to be understood and which lead to serious disputes. Knowing that they are issues of epistemology or methodology helps to sort out where they are different from related issues of ethics, politics or practical constraint, and where they overlap.

Epistemology and methodology in research on/for/with people

Epistemology, by whatever name, cannot be avoided, because 'epistemology' is the theory of knowledge, and research is, at least partly, about getting knowledge.[1] Epistemology encompasses a set of questions and issues about knowledge: what it is, how we get it, how we recognize it, how it relates to truth, how it is entangled with power. It is a difficult subject partly because it is self-referring: how can we know what theory of knowledge is the right one? It is also difficult because so many people take it for granted that they know what they know. So if they are challenged about *how* they know it, or even *whether* they really know it, it is hard for them to find the right terms in which to discuss the matter.

Methodology is an offshoot of this set of questions. It refers to the theory of getting knowledge, particularly in research contexts. It provides a rationale for the way in which a researcher goes about getting knowledge. It is more, therefore, than an account of particular techniques, such as 'using an interview' or 'doing a survey'. It provides reasons for using such techniques, in relation to the kind of knowledge that is being collected, developed or constructed – these different terms fit different theories of knowledge.[2]

Methodology is of particular importance in research about human beings. Unlike the physical sciences, educational research is always on/for/with other people – and getting knowledge on/for/with other people is a complex matter. It is complex for three main reasons: human agency; social relations, especially the effects of power; and ethics. The terms 'agency', 'power' and 'ethics' indicate that these questions are particularly significant for educational research for social justice, which, as I said in Chapter 1 (pages 12–13), is directly concerned with power, empowerment and the good of communities and individuals. My use of 'on/for/with' indicates that I include any or all three of these possibilities as a possible stance in any given piece of research. However, which of these stances is taken is of issue in the design or evaluation of research for social justice, because each of them carries implications of agency, power and ethics.

I shall point out how issues of methodology in educational research compare with such issues in the physical sciences. The argument could be extended to other sciences, such as astronomy, geology, biology or palaeontology. These are sciences which are more methodologically complex than physics, since the experimental method is more difficult to carry out, if not impossible, in all of them. Certainly, there are some concerns in these areas which usefully overlap with educational research, as the new work in complexity and artificial life is showing. However, my main concern here is the significance of human beings in educational research, and this is most sharply pointed up in relation to the physical sciences, which are so widely perceived as successful in their pursuit of knowledge.

First, human beings have agency. Unlike the objects of research in the physical sciences – crystals, electrons, atoms, fluids, electromagnetic fields – human beings are not simply passive subjects of research. All human beings react to situations, including the situations of being researchers or research subjects. In other words, they have agency: they can and do construct interpretations of events, and they can and do use such interpretations as reasons to act in particular ways. To put this another way, human beings construct meanings for the events in which they participate. This has a significant impact on what can be known about human beings (epistemology) and how anyone could come to know it (methodology).

The significance of agency in the human sciences can be shown using the example of repeating an experiment. Repetition is an indispensable part of the methods of the physical sciences. Repeating an experiment or test on an inanimate object should give the same result every time. Many experimental methods depend on this. Repetition is carried out by experimenters in the physical sciences because it improves the likelihood of getting a good result. The same is not true of repeating an experiment or test on a person. To take a particularly simple example, each time a billiard ball is bumped with a particular force it should behave in the same way. But imagine trying the experiment of bumping into a stranger on a bus to see what will happen. Then repeat the experiment, i.e. bump into the same person. And again. It would be very odd if the result remained the same all three times. Alternatively, bump into three similar people (judged by size and weight). Again, the result is likely to be different in each case – especially if any of them have seen you bump into anyone else. The repetition in this case constitutes a different act, even if it is still describable as 'bumping'. This is in sharp contrast to repeating the experiment of bumping a billiard ball three times. In educational research, as in all social science, it is customary to refer to 'replication' rather than 'repetition'. This terminology indicates the impossibility of exact repetition in any process to do with human beings.

The contrast between repetition and replication relates to epistemology (what can be known) and methodology (how to find it out). The reasons for the difference between the two kinds of experiment are bound up with the interpretations a person places on an action. If an experiment such as the one described showed anything, it would show something about the kinds of interpretations placed on such an event by the subjects. Thus, what could be known includes the interpretation, and how to find it could also include asking the people involved to explain their interpretations. Inevitably, the interpretations of the researcher form part of the method of producing the knowledge. These questions of human interpretations and how to discover them are not relevant in physical sciences, just as some of the kinds of knowledge and methods of physical sciences are of limited relevance in the human sciences. Wittgenstein (1968: 180) produced a neat example of the significance of the interpretations of the human beings involved in human sciences, whether as subjects or as researchers:

> I describe a psychological experiment: the apparatus, the questions of the experimenter, the actions and replies of the subject – and then I say that it is a scene in a play. – Now everything is different. So it will be said: if this experiment were described in the same way in a book on psychology, then the behaviour described would be understood as the expression of something mental just because it is *presupposed* that the subject is not taking us in, hasn't learnt the replies by heart, and other things of the kind.

I come back to the question of interpretation in relation to values in the next chapter.

Wittgenstein uses the idea of 'an experimenter', and this alerts us to another aspect of the kinds of interpretation that have to be taken into account in the human sciences. Social relations, and, in particular, the power relations inherent in any human interaction, are significant to what goes on in human situations. Even if the power is distributed equally, it is still a factor. Equality is a kind of relationship, and it needs to be taken into account. In most human relationships, however, the complexities of power relations are such that it is difficult for them to be straightforwardly 'equal', even if they are in some kind of balance. Clearly, this is an issue which must be significant for any educational researcher for social justice, since they will, precisely, be researching both on and in the context of unequal power relations: for instance, teachers and children; the hierarchies of educational institutions; the governance of education; social inclusion or exclusion.

A particularly clear example of the significance of power can be seen if Wittgenstein's example is taken to refer to the well known experiment by Milgram (1963), in which subjects were asked to administer electric shocks to other people. Milgram was researching into the phenomenon of obedience to authority. Unknown to the subjects of the experiment, actors had been asked to simulate the effects of the shocks. It is interesting that in a study on obedience to authority, the experiment was set up as a 'scientific' one, in which the subjects were being asked to participate in a piece of scientific research. In other words, the situation was deliberately set up so that the subjects were influenced by the power ascribed in Western societies to science and research. This power of researchers to get compliance from their subjects is always at issue in human sciences.

Further complication is introduced in relation to the sector of society from which researchers come, compared to those researched. To return to the example of bumping strangers, one could imagine repeating it with a different set of people (at Ascot, queuing for the dole, on the way to a football match etc.), with the researcher wearing different clothes, perhaps (dressed very expensively or poorly, in police or army uniform etc.), or using a team of researchers (old, young, female, male, black, Asian etc.). It is likely that such changes would be significant, though in what way, exactly, would be a matter for the empirical investigation. It is noticeable that researchers tend to come from a narrow sector of society, and this, in itself, will influence the kinds of knowledge that can be produced. The categories I have chosen to place in the brackets are recognizably related to the distribution of power in our society: to wealth, gender, race and the forces of the state. These are all crucial to research for social justice. They are precisely the issues discussed, in different ways, by Mehreen Mirza, Stephen Ball and Melanie Walker, and, indeed, in other pieces of their research writing by David Gillborn and Caroline Gipps. Gillborn explores the relationship of state policy to the increase of racism and racial inequalities (Gillborn 1995, 1997). Gipps undertakes similar explorations in respect of state policy and children with special needs or who live in poverty; and in respect of examination success and gender (Gipps 1993; Gipps and Murphy 1994). I return to the issue of the connections between power and knowledge in Chapter 4.

The issue of power in social interaction alerts us to the third reason why human sciences are significantly different from physical sciences. This is that ethical issues are always relevant where dealing with human beings is concerned. As I have said, research can be on/for/with human beings, and the categories 'on', 'for' and 'with' are ethical categories.[3] The distinction between the three does not apply to the physical objects which are studied in physical science. Thus, in the human sciences there are ethical issues which have methodological implications. This is something of no concern in physical sciences. In drawing this distinction I am only drawing attention to one set of ethical concerns. There are others which are shared by all researchers, including those in the physical sciences. A particularly obvious example of the latter is the ethical concern surrounding the uses to which knowledge can be put. This is as much a matter of concern in nuclear physics, for example, as it is in studies of race in education. However, such concerns have no methodological implications.

Ethics have methodological implications in research on/for/with human beings, especially where that research is explicitly intended to improve social justice. An example is the use of control groups. These are, methodologically, extremely useful if repetition is not possible. Thus, they are widely used in botanical experiments, in order to test the influence of a single factor on a population (of flowers, say, or beans). Agency and interpretation can be taken into account by the use of 'double blind' tests, where neither the experimenter nor the subject know which is the control group or treatment. For instance, much medical research depends on the double blind use of placebo treatments. The ethical problem for education (as for medicine, but not for botany) is that the method depends on putting some subjects into a 'control' group and deliberately giving treatment thought to be inferior so that better treatments can be tested. For example, in my own university department, colleagues have designed some research to test a method of classroom management by changing the seating in a classroom depending on the task set. Previous research has indicated that this technique has had a high degree of success in improving the achievement of the 'long tail' of low-achieving children in a range of different classrooms (Hastings and Schwieso 1995). This is research with the potential of benefiting children at a socio-economic disadvantage in educational terms, since it is those children who are disproportionately represented in the 'long tail' of under-achievement. An opportunity has arisen to test this further on a wider scale in a considerable number of schools in a nearby LEA, using other schools in the same authority as the control group. The research team had decided to limit what it believes is good practice to a few schools. It now faces another dilemma about how far to publicize the technique (which it believes in, and which it already has evidence for) through its teacher education courses, for instance, and through consultancies in the other schools in that LEA, particularly in schools in areas of multiple socio-economic disadvantage.

Ethical issues which are related to being 'on/for/with', and which are particularly relevant for social justice, are also raised by experiments or research methods that depend on deceiving the subjects. One famous example is the famous 'Pygmalian in the classroom' experiment on teacher expectations (Rosenthal and Jacobson 1968). In this experiment, teachers were given false information about the predicted educational success of pupils in their classes. The research demonstrated the subsequent strength of the teachers' expectations in determining the actual progress of the pupils. Another example is provided by my own research. In a survey into gender as a factor in the introduction of computers into primary schools (Griffiths and Alfrey 1989), the decision was taken to make it look as if the research was not particularly concerned with gender. For example, questions about gender were hidden in a number of other general questions in which we had no interest. Even more deceptively, the gender of the head and of the teacher responsible for the computer was found by asking for their name as 'Mr/Mrs/Miss' – though, in fact, we had no reason to want the name, which was deliberately left out of the coding for reasons of anonymity and confidentiality. This was a deliberate deception. It was, however, taken within an ethical framework. While I would defend this decision, it cannot be certain that I was right, as with most ethical dilemmas. Similarly, Stephen Ball, in his research into the micro-politics of the school, did not explain to his subjects that he would use the data within a theoretical framework focused on power and conflict, rather than on authority and consensus. This is less of a deliberate deception than mine was, but it is a kind of deception, none the less.

For anyone wanting to do educational research for social justice, resolutions to these ethical issues of deception depend on judgements about 'on/for/with'. In cases where research is 'on' one set of people but 'for/with' another, the identity of both sets is ethically and politically significant. Deceptions involved in participant observations provide a familiar example. Any research which is based on participant observation, and which sets out to investigate sexism or homophobia in schools, will make use of remarks passed in the hearing of the researcher, as well as those recorded in formal interviews. Being able to do this is a strength of participant observation. In their studies of masculinities in school, both Askew and Ross (1988) and Mac an Ghaill (1994) make use of informal observation, as well as formal interviews, to document the widespread use of phrases like 'He's a cissy' or 'sly; not real men'. These are phrases picked up from subjects of the study who would not have been particularly aware that their comments were being perceived as significant. This is research *on* the school communities *for/with* boys outside traditional norms of white, heterosexual masculinity. In contrast, Rogers's research into the experience of young lesbians at school draws only on the formal interviews with the subjects of her study, and not at all on informal data which must have been readily available to her, as 'the mother of a daughter who had identified as lesbian during her time at a mixed comprehensive school' (Rogers 1994: 31). She is, I take it, being careful to use only information that the young women were offering explicitly. They retained a degree of control over the information that was presented about them through knowing just what was to be used.

Another, related, kind of deception arises in relation to doing research as an 'insider but outsider' to the community being researched. To the extent that the researchers are insiders, they are drawing on the normal ground rules of reciprocity and trust that pertain for social interactions in the community. To the extent that being a researcher means using these ground rules for research purposes, there is a risk of exploitation and betrayal. Ways of overcoming such dilemmas are not always straightforward. Stephen Ball (1991: 181) discusses some of them in relation to interviewing teachers:

> One response might be to say that in dealing with sophisticated adults the matter of how much to disclose can be left to the respondent to decide. But things are not that simple. The skills of interviewing built up over a number of years give the researcher an edge. The respondents may find themselves manipulated into saying more than they intended.

A number of such issues related to insider–outsider research are pointed up in Mehreen Mirza's discussion of researching a community in which she has some claims to be an insider. As a South Asian British woman she could be called an insider, but in other ways, and particularly because she is a researcher, she could be called an outsider. She discusses what kind of reciprocity is justifiable in the relationship formed between the interviewer and the interviewee. Her respondents hoped she would explain where to find an Asian women's photography club, give advice on completing UCAS forms and intervene in a marriage proposal. For her, as in all research which depends on the research relationship looking like a relationship of friendship, there was a fine line to be trodden between 'giving a voice' to the subjects and betraying them.

These examples show that none of the issues is easy to resolve. The use of control groups, deception and betrayal, for instance, can be attacked on ethical grounds. Equally these methods can all be defended. The team designing the LEA research has made a principled compromise. The research is going ahead, as designed, but no rigorous attempt is being made to limit the 'natural' spread of the technique. The argument is that it is worthwhile to get some stronger evidence about the technique which justifies the use of control groups. On the other hand, any results are not going to be much affected by any other uptake of the technique, since that is likely to be patchy anyway. So in this case, there is not a strong enough reason to justify withholding information about what seems to be good practice from those who want to benefit from it.

Mehreen Mirza's discussion shows that she treads a delicate path in her research. On the one hand, her subjects were clear about what she was doing, and were happy to cooperate, as long as they remained anonymous. On the other hand, they almost certainly could not have had anything like a full understanding of what kind of evidence she was using, or what she would do with it. Some of their ethical assumptions were, as she shows, at odds with her own, especially with regard to how to act in mainstream, white, British society. Thus, the judgement she has had to make concerns how far she exercises her own ethical standards when drawing conclusions and acting on her research. These ethical standards are, precisely, related to the interactions of South Asian women with regard to mainstream, white, British society – and how far she respects their perspective on what would be ethically proper. It is interesting to note the similarities here with the dilemmas Melanie Walker wrestled with in South Africa, with regard to emancipatory intentions. It is also interesting to note the different conclusions reached in the two cases. Mehreen Mirza continued with her emancipatory anti-racist, anti-sexist intentions even when such intentions were at odds with the concerns of her subjects. Melanie Walker, on the other hand, needed to adjust her own emancipatory intentions as she realized that they had oppressive effects on her subjects. In my view, given the different social and historical contexts, the two researchers were right to reach different conclusions about what might otherwise seem to be similar cases.

In general, human agency, social and power relations and the significance of ethics complicate the business of getting knowledge on/for/with people. In human sciences in general, and in educational research in particular, all these issues are both pressing and difficult. There are no simple answers to these questions. They depend on the views the researcher holds about human beings and about ethics. These kinds of question hardly ever arise in sciences like physics or geology, which deal with inanimate objects. Epistemological and methodological considerations are relatively straight-forward in such sciences. It could even be said:

> In the twentieth century the unity-of-science thesis of the Vienna Circle provided the modern justification for prescribing a hierarchy of the sciences with physics at the top. Ironically, my analysis here can be understood to agree that the sciences should be unified – but I propose that the hierarchy should be 'stood on its head'. On scientific grounds, as well as for moral and political reasons, those social sciences that are most deeply critical and most comprehensively context-seeking can provide the best models for all scientific enquiry, including physics.[4]
>
> (Harding 1991: 98)

In Chapters 4 and 5 I look more closely at some of the dilemmas and debates produced by this epistemological and methodological entanglement with human beings. I discuss how the agency of human beings, their relationships with each other and the ethical questions that result have implications for debates about the questions of committed research. Must having a commitment to a political or ethical position adversely affect the research – or, on the contrary, will it improve it?

Notes

1 The word itself shows this: it comes from the Greek word 'episteme', meaning 'knowledge'.
2 For simplicity's sake, I give brief explanations of the key terms, 'methodology' and 'epistemology'. However, it is important for researchers coming new to the field to be aware that any brief explanation is bound to be partial. The exact meanings of terms like 'methodology', 'method' and 'technique' are inherently unstable, precisely because of the depth of argument about them. This situation can be confusing to anyone new to the field. If you, the reader, are feeling it is somehow your fault that you can't find one clear definition that works for everything you read, then you need to know that you can abandon the search. Instead, you need to develop an understanding of the range of use, and to be clear about your own understanding, as a result.
3 Ethical considerations of this kind are not applicable only to human beings. Experimentation on animals also raises ethical issues. This is because animals need to be treated with a care and consideration that is not needed for inanimate objects. To put this concretely, guinea pigs and rhesus monkeys can be hurt physically and psychologically, but rocks and metals cannot. (I do not know about worms and fish.) The treatment of animals is also relevant to the issue of justice and good communities, since communities can be understood as including other creatures besides human beings. But this debate is far beyond the scope of this book.
4 Charles Taylor puts forward a different but related argument in his project to locate naturalism within hermeneutical theory (Taylor 1985: 6). He argues that the naturalistic enquiry and the 'sciences of man' should use different methods, although, like Harding, he thinks that natural science is carried out in a value-laden context which explains it better than does its own self-understanding. There is more about natural science and social sciences, including some of Taylor's argument, in Chapter 4.

4 | Facts and values: power/knowledge

Epistemological and methodological issues in research for social justice

In Chapter 3, I discussed the significance for epistemology and methodology of human agency, of social interactions (especially the effects of power) and of ethics. I discussed the significance of the way human beings use their agency to interpret their worlds, and I discussed it in relation not only to the subjects of research, though this was important, but also to the researchers, who are themselves human beings. All this was shown to be of great importance for educational researchers interested in social justice.

In this chapter I take these issues further by considering how – or how far – values enter into interpretations: that is, if – or how far – facts can be value free. This is a matter which is crucial for anyone interested in research for social justice. It is also a matter which is widely and hotly debated both in and out of educational research communities, though I shall draw on education examples and theories as much as possible. These debates are subtle and complicated. They draw on a range of theoretical frameworks, none of which deals in easy answers. Educational researchers do not have the luxury of remaining within just one of these theoretical frameworks: the questions that arise in educational research necessitate some familiarity with several of them. As a result, this chapter is, inevitably, more dense and difficult than most of the others in the book. So some readers might like to skip it at first reading. Others will find it exactly the one they want to start with.

As I shall explain in this chapter, some researchers argue that facts are objective and unbiased if, and only if, they are not contaminated by values. They say that once the facts are established, values are brought into play in order to use the knowledge well: to make progress and to improve things. Against this, others would argue that such facts do not, and could not, exist. A particular facet of this debate is the place of power in the construction of values and knowledge, including, in some Foucauldian versions, the ethics underpinning the 'regimes of truth' which constitute knowledge in any particular society. One consequence of this position is a radical uncertainty about the very possibility of knowledge and truth. These are complex arguments, with more than two sides to them; scepticism about the possibility of reaching any objective facts or certain, universal truth comes from more than one theoretical position.

These debates can be unpicked into various related strands. Two debates in particular are addressed in this chapter: the relationship of facts and values; and the argument that knowledge is inextricably connected to power structures in society. These two debates are closely connected, but often seem (confusingly for anyone trying to engage with them) to take place in isolation from each other. One reason for this is that they tend to draw on different modes of arguing, sets of vocabulary and canonical theorists. In short, the debates draw on different discourses, but I am trying to bring them into a discursive relation with each other. I do this directly on pages 54–63, where I discuss different views about the relationship of power and knowledge, in relation to different approaches to knowledge. The discussion is continued in Chapter 5, where I consider the possibility of trying to gain knowledge and reach for justice in conditions of uncertainty and diversity, especially in relation to power.

The resolution of these debates is peculiarly urgent for the educational researchers to whom this book is addressed. As I said at the beginning of the book, research with an explicit ethical or political commitment needs to defend itself against the charge that it is biased and suspect from the start. ('You would say that wouldn't you.') Simultaneously, it needs to defend itself against the charge of naivety and co-option into precisely those structures of knowledge production which are themselves productive of injustice. ('You've sold out and become one of them.')

Facts and values: objectivity and interpretation

A four-sided debate

The debate about the relationship between facts and values underlies many of the arguments about committed research and its possible objectivity. This is a debate which is relevant to, but cuts across, other issues within research on/for/with human beings, such as the nature of power or the possibility of human progress.[1] It is not independent of these issues, but I shall begin by considering it on its own, before linking it to them. Although ethical values are included, it should be noted that 'values' include any evaluation, ethical or not, that something is good, bad or neither – or, indeed, beautiful, funny, disgusting, surprising or interesting, in so far as these cannot be subsumed under ethical evaluations of 'good' or 'bad'.

I start from the question of whether there must be a relationship between facts and values, or whether each is independent of the other. This is a many-sided debate, rather than the two-hander too often presented.[2] The history of this debate in Western modern times is one which has been strongly affected by the perceived success of the physical sciences in their search for knowledge. A search has been made for similar methods in the human sciences to provide objective knowledge, where 'objective' refers to independence from the particular observer who happened to produce it. The aim of these methods is to produce a kind of 'god's eye view': a formulation of knowledge which corresponds to an external reality. To put this into more everyday terms, the aim is to stick to the facts; to ascertain the facts of the case before making a judgement on it; or to discover what really happened, regardless of what particular individuals might think. Thus, the aim is not to deny the inevitability of interpretations in research on/for/with people, but for such interpretations themselves to be independent of a particular observer – and her value positions. The very possibility of being able to develop a 'god's eye view' has been denied by others, who search, instead, for methods which will provide knowledge without any such requirement. They include both those who think the methods of social science are very different from the human sciences, and those, like Harding, quoted at the end of Chapter 3, who think that most of those impressed by the methods of the physical sciences are working with an overly simple idea of all knowledge, including all scientific enquiry.

For simplicity, I consider the debate in terms of four points of view about facts and values. This is, inevitably, a schematic oversimplification, but some of the complexities will become apparent in the course of the chapter. From the first point of view, researchers expect to 'just stick to the facts' – where facts are *value* free (not just interpretation free). From the second point of view, researchers or users expect that value judgements will always bias research, but that the more such bias can be eliminated, the better the research. Yet a third point of view is taken by those (I am included here) who argue that all facts and information are value laden, but this is not helpfully described as 'bias', since in this context the sense of the term 'bias' depends on there being a possibility of a neutral view. This group argues that 'perspective' is a better description than 'bias', since knowledge of human beings gets its meaning from the value system of the knowers. A fourth point of view (and again this includes me) takes this further. Holders of this view are impressed by the political and social dimensions of individuals' value systems. Thus, for this group, knowledge gets its meaning from the political position of the knowers, as well as from other value systems.

Opinions and bias; universal and local knowledge

The contours of the debate are obscured by shadows looming from adjacent debates. It is important to recognize this, so as not to get deceived by the shadows into seeing things which are not there, or, conversely, into *not* seeing things which are. Two of the most significant of these adjacent debates are those concerning: (a) opinions and bias; (b) universalizable or local knowledge. I say something about both of these, before continuing with the main theme of the section. I come back to these issues in Part III.

Value judgements are often treated as if they are opinions which bias research. Researchers may expect to – or be asked to – find facts or information, and keep their opinions to themselves, or, at least, not allow them to affect the results of the investigation. This expectation is often confused with the expectation that researchers should keep their value positions to themselves. However, all serious researchers recognize the difference between opinion and knowledge – even if they disagree about how to identify each of them. Similarly, all serious researchers recognize the dangers of allowing dearly held opinions to affect the care with which unwelcome research results are treated. Bias exists, as I shall say later, in relation to the undue influence of opinion, but also especially from a lack of reflection on the values held by the researcher or research team. Thus, I shall argue, the removal of bias requires researchers to address their value positions, which therefore need to be explicitly stated as far as possible.

The difference between universal and local knowledge – of particular circumscribed situations – is another debate which gets confused with debates about fact and value. The difference between universal or local knowledge can also be described as the difference between widely applicable knowledge and knowledge which can only be of use as illumination of, or through partial similarity with, other situations. The confusion arises because it is often believed that the collection of unbiased, factual evidence is part of a larger research ideology of contributing to a joint venture of building up universalizable knowledge, piece by piece. It is further often believed that individual values and value judgements get no purchase in such an enterprise. Conversely, it is assumed that knowledge which is marked by individual values cannot be of any use in the project to build up such cumulative, universal knowledge. This is a confusion, because the possibility of accumulating knowledge is not necessarily contingent on the place of values in producing it. However, the arguments about one tend to get associated with arguments about the others. It is easy to see why: it is because of the relation of the fact and value debate to the debate about the uses of the methods of physics and the search for objective knowledge in human sciences. On the other hand, it is easy to find people on different sides of the fact/value debates who believe they are producing universal knowledge; and similarly with local knowledge. So if a relation exists between the two sets of issues, it has to be shown, rather than assumed.

The separation of fact and value

Having noted the shadows cast by these two debates, I return to the debate at issue in this section: fact and value. The first of the four points of view is that facts are value free. Arguments about fact and value have a long history in philosophy and in the theory of social science. They can usefully be traced back to the British empiricists, and to David Hume in particular. Hume was impressed by the success of natural science, and tried to apply similar methods to the project of developing a 'science of man' (Hume 1739: 42):

> The only solid foundation we can give to this science itself must be laid on experience and observation. It is no astonishing reflection to consider, that the application of experimental philosophy to moral subjects should come after that to natural, at the distance of above a whole century; . . .
>
> And though we must endeavour to render all our principles as universal as possible, by tracing up our experiments to the utmost, and explaining all effects from the simplest and fewest causes, it is still certain that we cannot go beyond experience.

His philosophy is uncompromising about the distinction between fact and value. His argument concerned evaluations to be found in what he called the passions (pride, humility, hatred and love), as well as in vice and virtue. These, he said, were independent of truth and falsehood:

> Truth or falsehood consists in an agreement or disagreement either to the real relations of ideas, or to real existence and matter of fact. . . . Now it is evident our passions, volitions, and actions, are not susceptible of any such agreement or disagreement.
>
> (Hume 1740, III.ii.1: 193)

Similarly, moral distinctions, he says, are derived from a moral sense, and have no relation at all with the facts of how the world is: 'Morality consists not in any relations, that are the object of science; but if examined, will prove with equal certainty, that it consists not in any *matter of fact*, which can be discovered by the understanding' (*ibid.*: 202). Such a sharp separation has as a corollary that statements about the objects of science – that is, anything that can be true or false – have no connection with morality, or with any other system of evaluation.

The empirical tradition has had a continuing influence, partly because of its foundation in 'natural science', and partly as convincing in its own right.[3] The empiricist turn can be traced in the nineteenth century through the inventor of sociology, Auguste Comte, who coined the term 'positivism' to describe a philosophy which emphasized the unity of the sciences, and to confine science to the observable and manipulable.[4] In the twentieth century, the group known as the Logical Positivists of the Vienna Circle emphasized observation by the senses, through the principles of verifiability: that some-thing is meaningful if and only if it is verifiable by observation through the senses. (In Karl Popper's well known version, this becomes modified into an analogous principle of falsifiability.)

From interpretations to definitions

The empirical tradition depends on keeping facts and values separate from each other. This is the position of the first point of view on what the relation-ship might be. The other three points of view share a belief that values are an inevitable part of the process of producing knowledge. They are distin-guished from each other by their views on how to deal with them: how far their effect can be minimized, and what kinds of values are to be taken into account.

Continuing with my schematic approach, I make no attempt to distin-guish all the many theoretical frameworks which are included in these three points of view. They include some which might be considered the heirs to the empiricist tradition, and others which are set up in opposition to it. For sim-plicity, I will put forward the bones of the arguments, with only the briefest references to the traditions from which they come.

In an analysis of Augustine's *Confessions,* Elbaz (1988) provides a useful discussion of fact and value from the point of view of critical theory. As he puts it, the distinction between facts and values relates to a logic of propo-sitions which 'conceals a static view of the world'. He explains:

> In other words, reality is assumed to be a homogeneous, consistent and non-changing phenomenon that can be verified ... The division between fact and value does not allow for the complexity of our social-ity. A fact is already an interpretation: interpretation is *sine qua non* to the possibility of language and communication.
>
> (Elbaz 1988: 29)

In support of this statement, Elbaz points out that even statements like 'It is raining outside' get their meaning from human interpretation. To take just one of the terms of the statement, the interpretation of the word 'rain' depends on, for instance, the need for a raincoat, or whether to take a bus instead of walking. Weather predictions are, in the end, referring to such a background context. His argument could be extended with further examples which would point up the significance of the human context. 'Rain' in a farming community would refer to planting or harvesting; in a holiday area, to the effect on any tourist behaviour. In the former case it would need to be relatively heavy to count; in the latter, relatively light. As we all recognize, these are not neutral contexts. They are contexts which are only compre-hensible in terms of evaluations, though in these cases ethically insignificant ones. Elbaz makes the argument for the term 'rain'. It is easy to see how the argument goes through even more easily for factual statements related directly to human beings. 'That is a child' or 'She is teaching them now' depend on an evaluation of who counts as a 'child' or what counts as 'teaching'. Even more obviously, statements like 'She is working class' or 'He is highly educated' are evaluative.

The question now arises as to how to deal with the evaluative content of factual statements. It is at this point that the second point of view parts company with the third and fourth. From this second point of view, it is hoped that the effect of values on factual statements can be minimized. One way of doing this is by devising definitions. Terms are derived from the ordinary human meanings, not the other way round. None the less, they can be made exact, and independent of further effects of human meaning. Meteorologists have particular definitions which decide when precipitation counts as rain (and not as drizzle, mist or sleet). From the second point of view, this is an excellent strategy. It may not be possible to get rid of the evaluations and the point in terms of human life, but it is possible to exhibit the assumptions as far as possible. It is likely, of course, that such a project could never be entirely possible, but that should not prevent the attempt. As for rain, equally for 'child' or 'teaching', 'working class' or 'highly educated'. A method can be agreed for defining each of these exactly, in order to lose the dependence on individual meanings ascribed to the terms. Such individual meanings may shift according to context, but within the terms of constructing knowledge, individual meanings must give way to the defined meaning.

Self-interpretation and multiple meanings

Those who take the third or fourth points of view find this argument simplistic, having, at best, limited use, as a special case. Elbaz himself argues that Augustine's *Confessions* can be understood in terms of church ideology disguising its values under the cloak of facts. He argues that Augustine's world view is rooted in the historical conditions of the fifth century, including the precarious condition of the Roman Empire and the shift from paganism to Christianity. Clearly, when there is widespread agreement in a community about an ideology, the context is relatively constant for different individuals in that community, and they can more easily come to an agreement. This is difficult when one community is trying to come to an understanding about another one. There is a well known debate about the existence of racism in schools which illustrates this. Peter Foster's (1990a) case study of Milltown High found little racism. This is in stark contrast to studies by Wright (1986) and Gillborn (1990). Gillborn (1995) convincingly argues that one of the reasons for this is that, unlike Wright and Gillborn, Foster prioritized an understanding of racism derived from the community of white teachers over the understanding derived from the community of

African-Caribbean students. The choice of one community over another is a matter for evaluation.

Charles Taylor provides a particularly clear statement of the significance of human values in producing knowledge about human beings. He argues that any point of view which ignores the context of values is inadequate, because it ignores the self-interpretation of human agents which are made in a context of distinctions of worth:

> The programme of naturalism as I define it above [i.e. using the natural sciences as a paradigm] is severely limited in principle. For there can be no absolute understanding of what we are as persons, and this in two obvious respects. A being who exists only in self-interpretation cannot be understood absolutely; and one who can only be understood against the background of distinctions of worth cannot be captured by a scientific language which essentially aspires to neutrality.
>
> (Taylor 1985: 3)

From this point of view, the gathering of data is severely limited in its use. Producing knowledge about human beings is, he argues, inevitably founded on readings of meanings. This requires insight, and it depends on formulating ways of talking about those meanings which explain, but do not predict, and which are, at root, moral sciences (*ibid.*: 52–7).

Human values are to be understood to include the values that underlie social systems, in particular political ones. Taylor goes on to draw connections between individual self-interpretation and the kinds of self-interpretations which are derived from public, social life. The points he makes are as relevant to the governance of education, and the assumptions underpinning it, as they are to the governance of society at large. He points out that our self-understandings are very different depending on whether we conceive ourselves as self-contracting individuals (as is common in the USA), or as participants in civic society sharing common ways of acting together (as was common in city states). The first of these is the self-understanding which underpins liberal society of the West, while the second underpins the civic republicanism of Machiavelli or Rousseau. Mary Midgley takes this theme up, too, in her recent discussion of the significance of agency and self-interpretation in the social sciences. Any interpretation of human actions, she argues, is marked by values about human agency and human self-understanding. Necessarily, this must include the interpretation itself, since it, too, is a human one. Thus, she argues that the systems for understanding physical, psychological or social behaviour of human beings select from view points, each of which is marked by an evaluative interpretation. These evaluations affect any research that is done, and in turn have moral and/or political consequences. Like Taylor, she points to the value position that underlies theories which are based on 'the myth of the original isolated, independent chooser needed for the Contract story'[5] (Midgley 1994:

113), and its connection to political individualism. She also uses the example of sociobiology to show how its reductionist values underpin its conclusions, which, in turn, underpin the moral and political project of finding technical, biological answers to moral and political questions. She quotes the sociobiologist E. O. Wilson on ethics: 'Only hard-won empirical knowledge of our biological nature will allow us to make optimum choices among the competing criteria of progress' (Midgley 1994: 73). This, she points out, is a politics in which management by experts replaces democratic consultation. Put into the context of education, educational research into school improvement is continually and necessarily faced with a choice of value positions, leading to expert management on the one hand or the possibilities of democratic consultation on the other. These are precisely the concerns underpinning the methodological choices in both Stephen Ball's and Melanie Walker's research, described in Chapter 2.

The significance of politics

Making the connection between values and political systems clears a path to the fourth point of view: that the political positions of knowers are significant factors in the construction of knowledge. This is something that neither Taylor nor Midgley includes as central to their arguments, although Midgley (1994: 113) does draw attention to it, remarking that neither of the central myths of individualism, Existential Man and Economic Man, 'easily accommodates a corresponding Woman'. Those holding to the fourth point of view argue that since self-understandings are influenced by political positionings such as 'woman' or 'man', this is indeed a significant factor in the relationship between facts and values. Thus, the fourth point of view is an extension of the third.

Two of the reasons for emphasizing the significance of political position are to be found as extensions of the arguments already discussed: the roots of language and communication in human contexts, and the effects of self-interpretation on human knowledge. First, the human context of communication and expression is, necessarily, shared. In other words, communication and expression depend on the existence of a public context, which itself depends on the participants agreeing on what kind of communication is going on. In Chapter 3, I quoted a thought-experiment from Wittgenstein which shows very clearly how the kinds of things that can be communicated in the context of a psychological experiment are different from those that can be communicated in other circumstances. The power of the psychologist is given by the 'conversation rules': the conventions which govern who may speak, when, about what and for how long. While some of these conventions are shared in any given society, others are different, depending on a participant's socio-political standing within the society. In general, conversation rules work to ensure that relatively high-status people are more likely to get their evaluations accepted. Decisions on whether to pay attention to high- or low-status people are decisions about whether to pay attention to meanings and interpretations of the relatively powerful or the relatively oppressed.

There are immediate implications in educational research. For instance, the difficult status of lesbian/gay/bisexual members of a school is partly brought about precisely because of their invisibility and lack of a public space. Arguments explaining this difficult negotiation of public spaces in the context of school are given by Epstein and Johnson (1994) and Mac an Ghaill (1994). The controversy about Foster's research into racism in Milltown High provides another example. It is not hard to see that it is relatively difficult for him to hear the points of view expressed by African-Caribbean pupils compared to the points of view of the teachers, who are of relatively higher status in the hierarchy of the school. But there is a political dimension here. Foster, I would argue, is implicitly taking a political, not simply an evaluative, position in relation to definitions and explanations of racism in his own research and in his criticisms of others. He is making the decision to give more weight to the expressed views of the powerful.

The difficulties of visibility and audibility can be overcome. It is possible, however, for alternative points of view to get heard. The conversation rules are not fixed for all times, all places and all social contexts, and meanings developed in one context can be brought into another. To take the example of gender, American research shows that women in single-sex groups talk with different conversation rules both from women in mixed-sex groups and from men in single-sex groups: they create a public space with different evaluative rules from those of men, both implicitly, with regard to the rules themselves (what a successful conversation is), and explicitly, with regard to the content of what is talked about. Women, then (like other socio-political groups, many of whom include women), have created a variety of meanings and evaluations – including the terms sexist and feminist.[6] These meanings and evaluations mark the beginnings of feminist, anti-racist or other alternative theory. Mehreen Mirza's work, as described in Chapter 2, could be said to contribute to new meanings drawn from those developed by British South Asian women.

The possibility of developing political consciousness is a second reason for the significance of socio-political position. This is an effect of self-interpretation, in that the self creates some of its identity by identifying with/as a social-political group. The action of joining or creating such a group in order to act together in itself affects self-interpretation. Any individual could, of course, be a member of an indeterminate number of such groups, based on socio-political factors of race, religion, sex etc. As Honig (1992: 226) puts it, 'A politics of performativity . . . generates "who" we are by episodically producing new identities.' Thus it is when, for instance, women, black people, lesbians, or any combination of these develop a political consciousness that it is possible to make something of these meanings, and for the gaps in 'standard' theory to get noticed and brought together systematically. These new meanings cannot be disentangled from a politics of position and intent. Any research into issues of gender, race, class or sexuality is inevitably political, therefore.

Alternative theory begins by pointing out serious gaps or inconsistencies in theories purporting to be theories of human beings, and suggests alternatives. Mehreen Mirza's anti-essentialist stance, described in Chapter 2, is intended as a contribution to such an alternative theory. A particularly resonant and famous example of an argument against 'standard' theorizing about human beings is Sojourner Truth's prose poem, 'Ain't I a woman', written in the middle of the nineteenth century, a poem which is the work of a black woman campaigning for both anti-slavery and equal rights for women:

> I have ploughed and planted and gathered into barns...and
>   ain't I a woman?
> I could work as much as any man (when I could get it) and
>   bear de lash as well
> and ain't I a woman?

Understanding power

Interpretations of power

By the end of the previous section, I was arguing for the relevance of power to questions of fact and value. I tried to show that some discussions of fact and value by-pass considerations of power altogether. However, I also presented the argument as a cumulative one, ending up with the relevance of power, because this reflects my own point of view. Obviously, anyone holding one of the other points of view would have presented this very differently.

The question of power is particularly significant in characterizing different stances on research for social justice. In introducing the issue, I talked of power relations and also of politics. In doing so, I knew I was talking vaguely because notions of 'power' and 'politics' are not clear or transparent. Rather, they are ambiguous and opaque. This is evident in the many different ways the words are used in everyday language, and also in the recent intense interest in theorizing power. So, just as I said that I was considering the fact and value question on its own as an analytical move, this section looks at power more directly, again as an analytical move. But it should be clear that I am still discussing the same basic questions of values and knowledge, bias and reliability. As in the previous section, the issues are relevant for education and also more widely. While some theories and their examples are drawn from education, others come from different social settings. They are, however, relevant to educational research, which would be the poorer if it had not drawn on and engaged with them.

In this section, I discuss some of the stances associated with research for social justice. I begin by outlining some of the theoretical underpinnings which have been provided for ideas of power. I discuss, *first*, liberal ideas, moving on, *second*, to Marxist-socialist ones and ending up, *third*, with currently influential discussions drawing on poststructuralist and postmodern analyses of power/knowledge and power relations. I divide the third category into two, focusing: (a) on the small-scale, especially as influenced by Foucault; and (b) on larger-scale effects of power relations. This is schematic,[7] but some of the complexities masked by the tidiness of the categories should become evident in the course of the discussion.

Liberalism and power

Liberal political theory is closely related to the empirical tradition discussed earlier. It retains its influence in theoretical writing and in everyday thinking of Western societies. The liberal analysis of power focuses on questions about the legitimation of authority in a just society. Indeed, the term 'authority' is preferred to that of 'power', as signifying legitimacy, with 'coercion' and 'force' being used to signify improper compulsion. In liberal theory, the authority to get somebody to do something is given by consent. This might be through an implicit social contract by which rational people agree to act on orders or to abide by the rules. There are two sources for such consent: first, procedural rules which ensure that 'each counts for one and no more than one' in rational arguments about what to do; second, an acknowledgement that some individuals have specialist knowledge, giving them particular authority in argument.

Knowledge holds a particularly important place in liberal politics. The concept of authority based on knowledge, and especially on specialist knowledge, is an important part of the liberal view of authority and power, because it underpins the hope of a rational use of knowledge to get control of the physical and social worlds. This idea is especially relevant in educational settings like schools and universities, because it underpins the authority and power which accrues to those possessing accredited knowledge. The liberal view is that those who have a command of knowledge can use it to advance their points of view. This can be done through argument and also through the authority that accrues to the possession of knowledge. Knowledge is powerful in argument, because, for liberals, it gets its force by its sure basis in empirical data. Along with this comes the further power of prediction and control of the natural and social worlds. There is thus a necessary ambiguity between technical and political power in the view that 'knowledge is power', a position held by both Bacon and Compte. Solving problems through technology has the merit of rational neutrality if the separation of fact and value is accepted. If it is not, however, there is a political imperative to distribute knowledge widely and on the basis of merit. This imperative underpins the political struggles to include working-class people, women and colonized peoples in the distribution of knowledge.

Marxist-radical critique

The liberal view of power has underpinned liberation movements, but it has also been criticized for its limits in respect of achieving justice. It was developed partly as a modern, emancipatory move against the legitimacy of sovereign or traditional power. It underpins theories of rights and civil liberties used by commoners, women and black people in their liberation struggles, including those for educational advancement based on merit.[8] However, it has also been criticized from a number of points of view for its systematic avoidance of questions of oppression and totalitarianism. It has been argued that the analysis may remain useful for some purposes, but that it is still narrowly focused on what can be achieved through the use of reason and arguments in a public debate by those who are able to articulate their needs and interests. Lukes's (1974) analysis and critique of conceptions of power in liberal theory is still one of the clearest. He points out that the pluralism of liberalism depends on a theory of power in which decisions about controversial issues take into account the views of individuals who want to influence the decisions. A development of this position is one in which power is exercised through 'the control over the agenda of politics and of the ways in which potential issues are kept out of the political process' (Lukes 1974: 21). This development removes the need for choices to be conscious, but retains the individualism of liberal pluralism. Thus, both forms of pluralism 'follow in the steps of Max Weber, for whom power was the probability of *individuals realising their wills* despite the resistance of others' (*ibid*.: 22).

For liberals, 'The bias of the system can be mobilised, recreated and reinforced in ways that are neither consciously chosen nor the intended result of particular individuals' choices' (*ibid*.: 21).

Lukes argues that this view of power is inadequate, because it does not take into account the power in social groups. The power they exercise is not an aggregate of the decisions of individuals in them. Further, the more powerful elite groups are able to persuade less powerful groups to hold views or to act in ways which are contrary to their own interests:

> To put the matter sharply, A may exercise power over B by getting him to do what he does not want to do, but he also exercises power over him by influencing, shaping or determining his very wants. Indeed, is it not

the supreme exercise of power to get another or others to have the desires you want them to have – that is, to secure their compliance by controlling their thoughts and desires?

(*ibid.*: 23)

This is a Marxist-radical critique[9] relevant to issues such as race and gender as much as to social class. Lukes himself uses examples drawn from both race and social class to make his argument. This critique also underpins Connolly's useful discussion of the politics of Foster's research and his differences with Wright and Gillborn (Connolly 1992). He points out the Weberian roots of Foster's stance and how it ignores the positions of 'domination and subordination that characterise social relations' (*ibid.*: 137).

The critique of liberalism is coherent with the view expressed on pages 53–4 that meanings and interpretations are developed in social groups which are themselves structured by socio-political power relations. Thus, since knowledge depends on human interpretation and values, research methods need to take the unequal power of social groups into account.

Research procedures have to be devised to take note of whose interests are being served, and what power structures underlie this. Various strategies have been suggested. Particularly influential these days, especially in anti-racist and postcolonial theory,[10] is Gramsci's idea of the organic intellectual who is both of and for a social group developing ideas through praxis. Gramsci (1971: 330) argued for the desirability of intellectuals who can work out and make coherent 'the principles and problems raised by the masses in their practical activity, thus constituting a cultural and social bloc.' He distinguished these from traditional intellectuals who 'put themselves forward as autonomous and independent of the dominant social group' (*ibid.*: 8). It is not enough, of course, simply to declare oneself 'organic'. Such an intellectual must remain in contact with the 'simple': that is, the non-intellectuals. However, this contact:

is not in order to restrict scientific activity and preserve unity at the low level of the masses, but precisely in order to construct an intellectual-moral bloc which can make politically possible the intellectual progress of the mass and not only of small intellectual groups.

(*ibid.*: 332–3)

In spite of their differences, there is a significant similarity between liberal, Marxist and some (but only some) radical conceptions of knowledge and power. All three concur in an Enlightenment hope of a rational use of knowledge to get control and progress in the physical and social worlds. This hope of using knowledge more rationally in order to improve the conditions of life is coherent with liberal and traditional Marxist-radical views that science will help to bring about emancipation, but finds itself at odds with some other radical views. Indeed, radical views now diverge between those that hold to universal emancipation as an ideal and those that argue for a more postmodern approach.

Poststructuralist and postmodern approaches

Both liberal and Marxist views of power have been the subject of critique from postmodern and poststructuralist writers[11] who are critical of the view that the rational use of knowledge is independent of the subject positions of the producers of knowledge. They are also critical of any attempt to bring about universal emancipation through the rational use of knowledge.

Michel Foucault is a particularly significant and influential figure in articulating this critique. In many books, lectures and interviews, he challenges the scope and adequacy of either of these views of power. He argues that, for all their differences, the liberal view and the Marxist or radical critique concur in focusing on the centralized power of the state in terms of a kind of 'economism'. He argues:

> I consider there to be a certain point in common between the juridical, and let us call it, liberal, conception of political power . . . and the Marxist conception . . . I would call this common point an economism in the theory of power. By that I mean in the case of the classic, juridical theory, power is taken to be a right, which one is able to possess like a commodity, and which one can, in consequence transfer or alienate . . . In the other case . . . power is conceived primarily in terms of the role it plays in the maintenance simultaneously of the relations of production and of a class domination which the development and specific forms of the forces of production have rendered possible.
>
> (Foucault 1980: 88)

He goes on to distinguish his own starting point as one which:

> should not concern itself with the regulated and legitimate forms of power in their central locations, with the general mechanisms through which they operate and the continual effects of these. On the contrary, it should be concerned with power at its extremities, in its ultimate destinations, with those points where it becomes capillary, that is, in its more regional and local forms and institutions.
>
> (*ibid.*: 96)

In challenging the scope and adequacy of earlier theories, Foucault is not claiming that his starting point will lead to an overarching theory of power. On the contrary, he says that he does not want to minimize the importance of state power, but simply to draw attention to the 'risk of overlooking all the mechanisms and effects of power which don't pass directly via the State apparatus' (*ibid.*: 73). He has also been criticized for focusing on domination and resistance to the exclusion of power exercised through consensus.

However, again, he disclaims an intention to create a complete theory: 'I have tried to indicate the limits of what I wanted to achieve . . . Consequently these analyses can in no way, to my mind, be equated with a general analytics of every possible power relation' (Rabinow 1984: 380).

A Foucauldian approach to power/knowledge is focused on the small scale, but, in general, postmodern critiques of emancipation are focused on a larger scale. Both approaches have been enormously influential for researchers interested in social justice. Equally, both have been enormously influenced by those researchers. In the case of Foucault's analyses, feminist and anti-racist researchers and scholars have energetically developed his analyses in the direction of research for social justice – and this in spite of his relative indifference to issues of social structures such as gender, race or even social class. In the case of larger-scale critiques, feminist and anti-racist scholars and researchers have formed an important part of the network of ideas and analyses, which, together, form the variety of theoretical positions referred to as 'postmodern'. In particular, they have shaped postmodern critiques of the possibility of neutral knowledge, and have used them in developing research for social justice.

While there have been some productive alliances between postmodernism and feminist/anti-racist research, it should be noted how uneasy this togetherness has been. I outline some of the reasons for this in my article on the subject, where I mention strategies of co-option and silencing, as well as some of the commonalities of the approaches (Griffiths 1995b). Anna Yeatman (1994: 187–8) summarizes the situation:[12]

> Postmodernism is a contested zone . . . For the former [i.e. those at the standpoint of the master subject contemplating issues of legitimacy for his authority] postmodernism is a general sea-change, reflecting the combined impacts of various social, cultural and technological changes. The revolt of the Other . . . remains unspecified and uninvestigated . . . From the standpoint of those who are contesting their status as Other, postmodernism appears as the efforts of the modern imperial, patriarchal master subject to manage the extent and direction of the crisis for his authority . . .
>
> Contemporary feminist theorists working within the politics of difference are making postmodernism over to their own agendas. This becomes a very different postmodernism from the quietist, pragmatic versions championed by such as Lyotard and Baudrillard. Postcolonial and feminist theorists of difference converge however in their insistence on a nexus between knowledge and power, and in their sustained contestation of how this nexus works to maintain and reproduce domination within modern social science.

With those cautions in mind, I go on to discuss very briefly how power is understood in these two ways of looking at the smaller and larger scale.

Two aspects of Foucault's theory have been particularly useful. One is the emphasis on locality and particularity. The other is the analysis of knowledge in terms of regimes of truth. In moving away from a consideration of power in terms of the state, he is able to move from thinking of repression – the power that says 'no' – to a power that is productive in a number of different ways, depending on the particular micro situations in which it is exercised. This means that it can exercise force and dominate more efficiently than a mere repressive force. On the other hand, resistance and power are not held by only one side. On the contrary, individuals 'are always in the position of simultaneously undergoing and exercising this power. They are always also the elements of its articulation . . . The individual which power has constituted is at the same time its vehicle' (Foucault 1980: 98). This is an analysis which has political and ethical consequences. Not only can this power and its productivity be distributed differently – 'We are not dealing with a sort of democratic or anarchic distribution of power through bodies' (*ibid*.: 99) – but also power can be used for good or ill, and needs to be used in articulation with 'rules of law, or rational techniques of government and of ethos, of practice of self and of freedom' (Foucault 1988: 18–19).

A particular productivity of power that is central to Foucault's work is the production of regimes of truth. Drawing on particular instances, such as institutions of psychiatry and education, he argues that procedures of power entering into play at basic levels are invested and annexed by more global phenomena, leading to the regimes of truth characterizing particular societies: 'Truth is a thing of this world: it is produced only by virtue of multiple forms of constraint. And it induces regular effects of power' (Foucault 1980: 131). In our own society, he argues, truth is characterized by the following traits: it is centred on the form of scientific discourse; it is subject to constant demands for economic and political reasons; and it is produced under the dominant control of just a few institutions, such as universities and the media. Thus, Foucault says:

> It's not a matter of emancipating truth from every system of power (which would be a chimera for truth is already power) but of detaching the power of truth from the forms of hegemony, social, economic and cultural, within which it operates at the present time.
>
> (*ibid*.: 133)

From a feminist and anti-racist perspective

Foucault considers the large scale, but only from a position grounded in the micro circulations of power. He is right that this procedure illuminates aspects of power hidden from more traditional approaches. However, Yeatman is right that, as with other postmodern theory, his method obscures particular effects of race and gender. As Haraway (1991: 236) also argues:

This is a central feminist criticism of Foucault's work: by highlighting the ubiquitous microcirculations of domination in his masterful analysis of the capillarity of power relations – that is, the constitution of resistance by power in a never-ending dialectic, and the demonstration of the impossibility of acquiring space without reproducing the domination named – he threatens to make the grand circulations of domination invisible.

It is precisely the effect of these 'grand circulations of domination' which has been the focus of feminist and anti-racist theory. At the end of the section on fact and values, I remarked on the significance of political positioning for the construction of knowledge. This came, I said, from (a) the effect of that positioning on language and communication and (b) the effects of a political self-interpretation on the construction of knowledge. This was a feminist argument, taken from my book on feminisms and the self (Griffiths 1995a). But it is not *only* a feminist argument, since similar ones arise from other areas of social exclusion: postcolonialism, anti-racism, queer theory. Looked at from the perspective of those who are socially excluded, the effects of political positionings are highly significant in the construction of knowledge.

The different theories which have been developed to take political positioning into account have been illuminated by Marxist (especially Gramscian) theories related to social class. They have also drawn on Foucault, Lacan and other postmodern perspectives. This cross-fertilization is the reason for the productive but uneasy alliances forged between postmodern theories and theories, like feminist ones, which start by challenging some of the 'grand circulations': the effects of gender, race, social class, sexuality and postcolonialism. For simplicity, I focus just on the example of feminism to show how feminist researchers have proceeded in producing well developed epistemological positions.

Since the early 1970s and earlier, feminist research has shown that there is a prevailing institutional sexism both in and out of formal institutions: educational institutions, including schools and universities; science and technology; social sciences; welfare policy; development policy (the list could continue for a long time). This research was largely carried out by women as a result of their self-conscious commitment to feminism. Previous research, carried out largely by men, had failed to show up this prevailing tendency. This created epistemological problems. How could knowledge be gender sensitive in this way? Was it perhaps that the results were just biased? Twenty years ago there was very little available analysis which could deal with the possibility that the political subjectivity of the knower in terms of her or his gender was relevant to the knowledge which was constructed. So there was no available theory to decide the validity or reliability of such new approaches to knowledge, other than to deny their respectability. The kinds of theory of power and knowledge that were available could, at best, offer partial discussions (e.g. in terms of sex-class), or, at worst, simply deny the possibility that knowledge could be other than neutral.

Feminists began by offering critiques of mainstream epistemology. They argued that such mainstream work can be interpreted as male-defined theory, in that it is an abstraction from the experiences and subject positions of males. The critique says that mainstream theory takes no account of the experiences and subjectivity of others, in that it is assumed by the producers of the knowledge that others are much like themselves, and there is no need to listen to their particular viewpoints. However, there was no need for the argument to stop short once a critique had been made. On the contrary, since we share some, but only some, of our viewpoints with both traditional producers of knowledge and those who have been previously marginalized, it was possible to use critiques of traditional views as a springboard to construct new ones.

The result was an explosion of theorizing in feminist epistemology, based around the ideas of subjectivity, personal and political identity, experience and political commitment. In consequence, there has been a continuing development of debates and recommendations about positionality, standpoint epistemology, situated knowledges and the relevance of postmodernism.[13] And, of course, there are serious differences between the various kinds of feminist epistemologies. Some of the theorists drew strongly from traditions of Lacanian psychoanalysis or from Derridean deconstruction.[14] Some leant more towards a kind of Marxist position of more certain, less biased knowledge that can be produced by reflection on position, producing what became known as 'standpoint theory'. Others again drew more eclectically from several of these sources. One of these, Donna Haraway, has done this in developing what she calls 'situated knowledge' – knowledge that is inherently fragmented and will never lead to certainty:

> Situated knowledges are particularly powerful tools to produce maps of consciousness for people who have been inscribed within the marked categories of race and sex that have been so exuberantly produced in the histories of masculinist, racist, and colonialist dominations.
>
> (Haraway 1991: 111)

These situated knowledges can be partially shared 'among very different – and over-differentiated – communities', sharing the 'web of connections called solidarity in politics and shared conversations in epistemology' (*ibid.*: 191), but never becoming the impersonal 'view from nowhere'.[15]

I have discussed feminist epistemology very briefly. Similar stories can be told for other or related areas of exclusion. Indeed, increasingly the different theories draw on each other, or produce syntheses. It should not be thought that these form a consensus, for they certainly do not, but still there are points of agreement. As Kathleen Lennon and Margaret Whitford (1994: 1) say by way of introduction to a collection of diverse essays on feminist perspectives in epistemology:

Feminism's most compelling insight lies in the connections it has made between knowledge and power . . . Work within feminist epistemology therefore shares preoccupations and critical moments with other important strands of recent thought: Marxists, southern scholars, theorists of what is now called postmodernism.

These diverse theories agree on the importance of position, of subjectivity, of political engagement. Thus they are all in stark contrast to those theories which insist on the separation of fact and value, power and knowledge, knower and known. Against this, all of them insist that knowledge is more reliable and valid precisely in the acknowledgement of its entanglement with individuals who are themselves positioned by gender, race, class and sexuality.

The discussion in this chapter has been dense and difficult, as I said it would be. This is partly because of the depth of differences of views about power and knowledge. I have illustrated some of this depth by allusion to the debate about the validity of some research studies about gender and race (Foster 1990b, 1991, 1992; Wright 1990; Connolly 1992). I alluded to Connolly's argument, which usefully picks up on the role of power and politics in this argument, and the way in which different understandings of it made the arguments incommensurable and interminable.[16] In the next chapter, I locate all this more securely in educational research. Then I come back to the question of power and how it 'should' be used, and also of knowledge and uncertain knowledge in the context of research in educational settings.

Notes

1 I used the formulation on/for/with in Chapter 3 to indicate different possible research modes in relation to human beings.

2 See the tables, common in introductory texts, putting all the attributes of methodologies on different sides, e.g. positivist, quantitative, analytic on one side, and humanist, qualitative, holistic on the other. But the divisions are not so neat, as a look at real research shows rather quickly.

3 Charles Taylor (1985, 1989) carefully traces the attractions of natural science owing to its unvoiced value systems. He summarizes the position: 'But what I am offering here is an account of the appeal of naturalism . . . it is the hold of a particular set of background distinctions of worth, those of the disengaged identity, which leads people to espouse what are ultimately rather implausible epistemological doctrines' (Taylor 1985: 6).

4 I have been careful to avoid the general term 'positivism', which is vague and unhelpful, especially as it is so often used pejoratively. On the other hand, it can be used, with precision, to refer to the Logical Positivists of the Vienna Circle. There is a useful account of the word in Hammersley (1995).

5 When Midgley refers to 'the Contract story', she is referring to 'The Social Contract'. This is a concept which has been used by political theorists, beginning with Hobbes and including Rousseau (who wrote a book called *The Social Contract*), to help to explain the workings of civil society. As Pateman (1988: 1)

puts it: 'The most famous and influential political story of modern times is found in the writings of the social contract theorists . . . The explanation for the binding authority of the state and civil law, and for the legitimacy of modern civil government is to be found by treating our society as if it had originated in a contract.'

6 I discuss this in more detail in *The Web of Identity* (Griffiths 1995a), as part of a discussion of language and its place in explaining the social construction of gender. I argue that it does, indeed, contribute to the construction of sexist, racist and class-ridden formations. But I also argue that the seeds of resistance and change are to be found in the alternative linguistic constructions to be found among groups of women, black people and working-class people.

7 For instance, it misses out other conceptions of power, such as that to be found in Arendt (where it is defined in contradistinction to force and domination). It also misses out all the subtleties of debate among liberals and among radicals. For instance, see Raphael (1976) for a useful overview of liberal debates. Evans (1982) is a useful introduction to some of the complex debates between Marxism and feminism.

8 Famous examples include Tom Paine, Mary Wollstonecraft and Martin Luther King.

9 Although it is not so often labelled as such, since both 'Marxism' and 'socialism' have become less fashionable descriptions than they were.

10 See, for instance, the whole tradition of the confusingly named 'subaltern studies' (Said 1978, 1993; Spivak 1988, 1990; Siraj-Blatchford 1994). The term 'subaltern' originates with a translation from Gramsci's Italian, where it simply means something like 'underclass'. The connection with the term as used in the British Army is unfortunate, especially as subalterns came from the ruling officer class.

11 Another caution is related to the terms poststructuralist and postmodern. I am not distinguishing them here. Lather (1994: 54) notes that they 'are often used interchangeably, driving some cultural theorists to distraction. Whole books have been written on this topic.'

12 Although I disagree with her about Lyotard.

13 The terms 'positionality', 'standpoint epistemology' and 'situated knowledges' have precise meanings in different feminist epistemologies.

14 Lacan and Derrida are both highly influential figures in modern French theory. Lacan's psychoanalytic school was strongly influenced by a linguistic interpretation of Freud. He is well known for his discussion of the 'mirror' stage of development. Derrida's philosophical work is also linguistic. His method of deconstruction and his concept of '*différance*' are particularly influential in cultural studies and the humanities.

15 I describe some of these in Griffiths (1995a). See also Harding (1991), quoted at the end of Chapter 3. There are excellent (but disagreeing) discussions in Rose (1994) and Stanley (1990).

16 This is reminiscent of Kierkegaard's (1843) discussion of the story of Abraham, who was commanded by God to kill his son Isaac as a sacrifice. Kierkegaard's analysis demonstrates that there is more than one way to tell this story, depending on the teller's faith. These tellings are not reducible to one another: descriptions in terms of sacrifice are incommensurable and untranslatable into descriptions in terms of killing or murder.

5 | Living with uncertainty in educational research

In Chapters 3 and 4 I have been summarizing and discussing some of the main debates underlying questions for educational researchers for social justice. It is all very well explaining debates, but they can become interminable. It is true that my discussion was not from a neutral position. (My argument was that such a thing is not possible anyway.) But this is a book subtitled 'Getting off the fence', and this chapter is where I move from leaning to one side to making the jump (while still acknowledging that others have jumped in other ways for defensible reasons). That is, I take a particular view of educational research. I also build on the epistemological position which I leant towards in Chapter 4 to argue that educational research remains possible and worthwhile even in conditions of diversity and uncertainty. My analysis, rooted as it is in a consciousness of those conditions, is strongly influenced by the collection of views which have come to be labelled 'postmodern'. Some configurations of 'postmodernism' have been widely taken to entail an 'anything goes' relativism of values and knowledge. Therefore, my argument requires me to discuss how it is possible to entertain the possibility of postmodern ethics and politics. To this end, I discuss the construction of uncertain knowledge and the fallible struggle for justice, especially in the context of educational research.

Educational research and other social sciences

Previous chapters have focused widely on human and social sciences, including, of course, education. In this chapter, I focus more closely on educational research.[1] So I begin by explaining what I understand by educational research. It might be thought that educational research was easily defined by its subject matter, or, perhaps, by the institutions in which it is carried out. However, the situation is not so straightforward. Education draws on and contributes to a wide range of academic disciplines in the human and social sciences, including history, law, linguistics, management, philosophy, psychology, sociology and social psychology. Thus, there are a large number of possible research fields related to educational contexts: learning, child development, acquisition of competencies, socialization and human resource management are all examples. Further, there are institutions outside academia interested in researching aspects of education. They include central government, local government, industry and various pressure groups. All this research may be relevant to people engaged in education, though it need not be. I would argue that only some of this vast array of research is *educational* research. There is more to educational research than a focus on subject matter.

The word 'education' is itself value laden: it is something which carries in its meaning a reference to good of some kind. This is so whatever might be thought of particular systems and arrangements for education, which are typically criticized for perverting education, which remains a good. Thus, to undertake educational research (rather than research in an educational setting) is to work within an ethical framework. This is so even if the ethical force of the term is unacknowledged.

The set of (positive) values – the good – which is indicated by the term 'education' has consequences for educational research. Thus, educational research is carried out in order to improve the education of children and students; and the term 'improvement' implies that there are particular factors which would be evaluated positively and others which would not. However, it is not obvious which set of values underlies such 'improvement'. Indeed, they are contested – not surprisingly, related as they are to wider systems of values and political positions (hence some of the reason for the interminable nature of debates about what is to be done in education). For this reason, I find it necessary to explain something of my own view of education and educational values, at least in outline. This gives me a basis to indicate the scope of educational research, and then to go on to discuss how such values affect research.

In my view, 'educational' entails the following: learning, criticality, an opening out; and all this in a way which is personal and interpersonal, and which fits the learners for life in wider society. This is a process which allows learners – and teachers – to change and develop their self-identities in ways that may be risky, but not to the extent of serious damage. Thus, education is concerned with both individual and collective well-being. It is highly personal and individual, and also highly social, political and public. To put this another way, education can only be understood as a practice, in a particular social and historical context, but it also depends on the uniqueness of personal relationships, constructed as they are within social and political structures. That is, teaching and learning depend on personal responses to the timbre of a voice, to a way of catching an eye, to a sense of humour or to a habit of bodily posture. Equally, teaching and learning depend on the social-political identities (of class, gender, race, sexuality, religion etc.) of the individuals involved (although we should note that such apparently personal traits as voice, glances, humour and posture are influenced by socio-political factors, and vice versa). Thus, both uniqueness and context are necessary parts of developing practice.

There are implications for, and effects on, research. First, educational research lays no claim to abstract neutrality or to being a curiosity-driven search for knowledge, of the sort that, for instance, sociology, history or philosophy might profess. Rather, in the long run (and sometimes in the short run), it is action-oriented. So it follows that educational research is not necessarily research *about* education or its processes. Rather, it is research which has an *effect on* education. It *participates in* the development of educational practices, whether that is directly in schools and classrooms or more broadly in policy or through initial teacher education. To use Wilfred Carr's formulation, it is *for* education, in both senses of 'for': 'on behalf of' and 'on the side of' (Carr 1997).[2] In particular, educational research is not identified with research *in* or *on* educational institutions, although, not surprisingly, much of it is indeed carried out in such places. However, educational research may not be focused on formal educational institutions at all.

Second, educational research is aiming not just at improvement, but also at personal and political improvement. Therefore, there must be a strong ethical and political underpinning to the framing of any research which is undertaken. That is, education is an area of research in which any changes that are sought are ones in which *both* individual (personal and ethical) *and* collective (public and political) changes are implicated. So educational research is research which participates in both personal and political changes. In short, educational research not only is action-oriented, but also cannot escape ethical and political issues. Nor should it try to, for such issues are logically implicated in its nature. This is why it is crucial to acknowledge the significance of ethical and political values, and why the debates about values, power and knowledge are always particularly relevant in educational research.[3]

To say that research is action-oriented does not imply any particular method or methodology. It is important to emphasize this, since a feature of this book is that it does not advocate any particular methodology (not even qualitative methodology) as being *the* right one for researchers in social justice. An extraordinarily wide range of research can be drawn on to improve education. Some of this is immediate: short-term, small-scale, action research is an example. This kind of action-oriented research is not the only possibility, however; nor need the effect be so immediate. Educational research can perform a range of functions, all contributing to the improvement of education, and achieve them through a variety of methods. Some examples of the functions of educational research include: asking the hard questions; providing facts; testing ideas and practices; testing hypotheses;

providing evidence; illuminating unseen areas; clarifying issues; and suggesting and evaluating new practices based on research. Examples of methods of research include: surveys; observational studies; information gathering; philosophizing; illuminative studies through interviewing and ethnographies; action research (in all its variety); production of materials; journal keeping; and critical reflection.

Some forms of action-oriented research are intended to have immediate, if local, effect, including, again, short-term, small-scale action research. Melanie Walker's research is in this tradition. Stephen Ball's research, on the other hand, has no such ambition. It is intended as a contribution to the theory of school organization, and as a way of changing some of the terms of that theory. However, he is clear about the politics of this theory, and clearly intends it to have a wider effect on the practice of schooling, as its ending (quoted in Chapter 2) shows. Melanie Walker, too, makes it clear that she wants her research to contribute to theory, partly by changing the terms of the kinds of collective political action available in educational change in South Africa. Both these pieces of research are action-oriented in this sense too. The social justice project I describe in Chapter 2 is also intended to be action-oriented in both these ways. It was designed so that the co-researchers could start making a difference in practice, in their various contexts, immediately. At the same time, it is intended to contribute to theorizing about social justice in education, and to have an influence on education through that route, too. To look ahead for a moment, my argument here constitutes a position in the debate about educational research and impact. I give a brief overview of this debate later in this section.

Just as no particular *method* is implied, neither is any research *context*, be it school, university or policy-making centre. All the kinds of research I listed can be – and are – done by teachers who, whether or not they have any formal research training, have a deep understanding of what to do in schools and classrooms. The same is true for other practitioners in education: advisors, tutors, LEA officials, governors, union officials and parents. At the same time, all of them can be – and are – also done with a high level of sophistication by career researchers, whether or not they have a deep understanding of school teaching and learning in practice. Doing research is not the sole prerogative of teachers, university researchers or policy-makers. The kind of research that can be done by each sector, however, depends on the particular constraints and motivations operating in the circumstances. These are very different for schools, higher education or government. Thus, all these kinds of research can be done – and in my view they should be – as part of a shared enterprise between people in different sectors of education, with different experience and skills related to education and research.[4]

This question of the proper purposes and ethics of educational research is the subject of lively debate in the educational research community, in Britain as elsewhere. It is a debate remarkable for the way in which it *is* a debate, rather than just a series of articles or books expressing positions.[5] This variety of view points is, of course, to be welcomed as fruitful. Just as educational research can borrow from other areas, such as philosophy, sociology or applied social science, it can also benefit from work carried out under different assumptions about educational research. I summarize briefly, before going on to develop my own position in the rest of the chapter.

Some themes recur in the recent set of debates. There are those who do not think educational research is action-oriented, but more like other academic subjects: a field of disinterested enquiry, using the same methods, and subject to the same criteria, as them. Ruth Jonathon (1995) and Alan Bryman and Robert Burgess (1994) seem to take this view in relation to the relationship of educational research to philosophy and social sciences, respectively. Martyn Hammersley is another exponent of the view that education is a phenomenon like others in social sciences; in his view, such phenomena are to be studied empirically in search of the truth and for the furtherment of knowledge (Hammersley 1995). Jenny Ozga sees the importance of education as 'a place where significant social science disciplines intersect' (quoted in Ranson 1996: 529). Others think that it is a hybrid drawing on other fields, and constructed from their intersection in the focus on education (see Ranson 1996). Against this, there are those who think that education can best be understood not as a phenomenon to be studied, but as a practice to be entered into. This requires attention to a particular social and historical context, and to individual personal relationships in all their anarchic variety (e.g. from a diverse set of methodological perspectives, Mac an Ghaill 1991, 1994; Weiner 1994; Hogan 1995; Carr 1997). Yet others see it as a field brought together by its focus on the central concept of learning, not necessarily in relation to students and teachers. The idea of a learning society is central here, as Ranson (1996) argues.

There is widespread (though not universal) agreement that educational research is concerned with improvement of the practices of education. The link with social justice is crucial here, because of the necessary, though too often inexplicit, relation between concepts of social justice and concepts of what counts as an improvement. It is not surprising, then, that the question of how the practice of research relates to the accomplishment or realization of any improvement is the subject of continuing, passionate interest. This can be seen in the ways in which successive British Educational Research Association (BERA) presidents have addressed the association on the question of how research should contribute to educational improvement over the past decade and more:

> It is our task as researchers, to use our relative detachment from the most extreme consequences of current policy, to provide the analysis that must be the first stage in any effective response.
>
> (Broadfoot 1988: 14)

Educational research is a form of practical inquiry which fuses inquiry with practice. There can be no educational research if teachers play no important role in the process of articulating, analysing and hypothesising solutions to complex educational problems. The specialist inquiries of professional researchers should be viewed as subordinate to this fundamental process.

(Elliott 1990: 16)

We want to ensure that the educational architecture is informed by our basic principles and research findings, and while politicians will always hold the aces we will have a say in what counts as an ace.

(Brown 1991: 7)

For me these are the key concepts in relation to professional educational research: the conduct and claims of the research need to be open to public scrutiny and criticism; the enquiry must be systematic, with all the complex requirements that that entails; the purpose must be to improve our theoretical understanding; and it should usefully inform the development of educational practice.

(McIntyre 1997: 133)

As these quotations show, there may be widespread agreement, but underlying it lurks a many-sided controversy about the kind of improvement wanted and the kinds of accountability that are entailed. In one corner, led by David Hargreaves (1996), there are claims that educational research should be judged by its immediate and general impact on practice. Responses to this have included arguments that judging research by its immediate impact in the way suggested by Hargreaves would be counter-productive (Hammersley 1997; McIntyre 1997). From another corner comes Ranson's (1996) article, which emphasizes the importance of impact, but primarily on theory rather than directly on practice, with the long-term goal of changing practice by developing theory in order to broaden the conception of learning and pedagogic practice. In yet another corner, there are claims that research should be judged by criteria related to its being educational or educative of the people directly involved in carrying it out, or, at least, to developing their personal knowledge (Whitehead 1993; O'Hanlon 1995). Critics respond that such research might have its uses, but is likely to remain not only local but parochial and introverted in its assumptions and effects, especially in relation to difficult political issues of social justice; and that educational researchers have wider responsibilities to students (Weiner 1989).

The debates are both complex and fruitful. As Ranson comments:

Intellectual controversy and uncertainty is the chronic condition of the post-modern world . . . Educational research, no less than other academic disciplines, has in recent years been influenced by this wider discourse and the epistemological uncertainties it has produced. There has been a lively and sometimes agitated debate between the traditions within educational studies about its status and forms of inquiry . . . Any discipline which is not critically re-evaluating the very foundations of its work, and whether 'foundations' are any longer possible, is vulnerable to the charge of intellectual closure and ossification. That educational studies has engaged in a public debate about its research must be considered a considerable virtue which others might emulate.

(Ranson 1996: 528)

Picking a way forward

I have argued that educational research is *for* improvement, *for* education. The question arises, however, whether improvement is possible; or whether in hoping for improvement we are deluding ourselves. The question is how to pick a way forward through the difficult terrain that characterizes educational research, especially educational research for social justice.

In Chapter 4, I said that research with an explicit ethical or political commitment needs to defend itself against the charge that it is biased and suspect from the start; and that, simultaneously, it needs to defend itself against the charge of naivety and co-option into precisely those structures of knowledge production which are themselves productive of injustice. I now take this further by considering charges against research for social justice, not only of bias and naivety, but also of paternalism, or, worse, in its aspirations to get improvement: that is, to work for justice. Thus, the debates are significant for those researchers who (a) begin with a clear set of values, (b) are concerned with power, be it empowerment of people or reducing their oppression, or (c) want to improve matters without imposing any one view of progress. Many researchers for social justice fall into all these categories.

Can knowledge be used to make progress? This question has become unavoidable, given the influence of the kinds of poststructuralist, postmodern and feminist positions outlined towards the end of Chapter 4, which implicated knowledge in oppressive structures. Of course, the issue has a particular significance for anyone reaching for justice – which is, inevitably, to reach for improvement in a particular situation with regard to inequality in the social distribution of power and resources. (See Chapter 1, page 13, and also Chapter 6, where I give an account of the nature of social justice.) The issue is also significant for all researchers working for any improvement at all. All educational researchers need to be aware of the strength of the different arguments, even if they have not been convinced by arguments which cast doubt on the neutrality and certainty of knowledge. In Chapter 1, I quoted Martyn Hammersley, who is well known for his arguments in favour of 'two cheers for positivism' (e.g. Hammersley 1995), discussing doubts about the capacity of research to produce neutral and certain knowledge. He argues, correctly, that continuing the debate is essential, because the issues (like the issues underlying the positivist position) are serious ones, with no easy answers.

Before continuing with the argument, I recap very briefly on some of the main points of the last section of Chapter 4, reformulating them a little in order to summarize them effectively.

1 The hope of accumulating *certain knowledge* has been widely (though not universally) lost. Under some feminist, anti-racist and/or postmodern formulations, such hopes have been discredited as being related to dismantling 'the master's house using the master's tools' (Lorde 1984); in others, as a result of a deconstruction of 'meta-narratives' of progress, on the grounds that such narratives mask their own entanglement with values and politics.
2 There are doubts about *knowledge being used well*, because of the way it is implicated in the circulation of power.
3 There are doubts about developing any *'god's eye view'* of the world, because all knowledge is perspectival and situated, bearing the marks of the knowers.

These arguments have implications for there being a possibility of improvement through research. As explained in Chapter 4, different views of good research are often incompatible. Indeed, the language of progress and improvement is itself in question, with many of the different formulations being themselves incompatible. At one extreme, there is the march of progress looked for in Bacon's and then Comte's hope that knowledge would lead to rational control. Postmodern perspectives are very different, especially for those who do not take the 'post' of 'postmodern' to be a temporal statement.[6] Rustin (1995: 24)expresses this clearly: ' "Progress", in this perspective, might be measured not by our distance from the "premodern" past, but by the extent to which its diversity becomes a cultural resource for us. This view is not without its appeal.' To look forward in the argument for a moment, it seems that ideas of improvement may still be usable, even if not part of a grand narrative of progress. However, this is to go too fast, because there are several stages in the argument to be considered first.

Even if there is a sense of 'improvement' which does not rely on a temporal march of progress, there is still the question of uncertainty and diversity in what can be known and what is of value. If there is such uncertainty about what can be known to be true and right, the question arises in what sense, if any, knowledge can be used to change a situation, and in what sense that change can usefully be called an improvement. This is, of course, the old dilemma of relativism in new clothes. These days, it most often presents itself in postmodern guise. It is often asserted that the postmodern turn is inimical to projects like social justice, because they are Enlightenment projects which aim at improvement of the human condition through knowledge and reason. In what follows, I argue that this assertion is mistaken. *First*, I show that the postmodern turn is not necessarily inimical to the Enlightenment project which is said to underlie movements of social justice. *Second*, I discuss the possibilities of holding to values in postmodernism, even given its rejection of any 'meta-narratives'. Then, *third*, very briefly, I relate the theoretical argument to actual cases of educational practice and educational research.[7]

The first problem is the apparent theoretical incongruence between the Enlightenment project and its various critics. The battle between old-style Enlightenment theorists and their postmodern critics has been entertainingly described by Kate Soper (1993: 21):

> A caricature [of the dispute] presents us on the one side with the dogged metaphysicians, a fierce and burly crew, stalwartly defending various bedrocks and foundations by means of an assortment of trusty but clankingly mechanical concepts such as 'class', 'materialism', 'humanism' . . . Obsolete as these weapons are, they have the one distinct advantage that in all the dust thrown up by the flailing around with them the wielders do not realise how seldom they connect with the opposition. On the other side stands the opposition, the feline ironists and revellers in relativism, dancing lightheartedly upon the waters of *différance*, deflecting all foundationalist blows with adroitly directed ludic laser beams.

Soper herself uses this caricature to deconstruct the dichotomy which underlies it – while aligning herself, if she has to, with the growling metaphysicians.

A very similar battle used to be seen raging on the field of education. It can be found for instance, in the work of Skeggs (1991), Troyna (1993), McLaren (1994) and Hammersley (1995) – growling from very different metaphysical positions.[8] The growling that is of particular interest here is against the inherent political conservatism that accompanies some of the postmodern dances. Some of the attack was issued as a warning to those who thought to use postmodern thought without seeing the dangers of such conservatism. There are indeed dangers, though they are sometimes less than critics fear. As Usher and Edwards (1994: 223) argue (rather seriously):[9]

> The postmodern, then, is criticised by both neo-conservatives and progressives and nowhere is this more the case than in its ludic manifestations . . . Attempts have been made to distinguish the 'serious' and ludic aspects of the postmodern. The 'serious' moments are equated with resistance and appropriated for their critical purchase on the postmodern moment, while the ludic are dismissed as a succumbing to the

consumerism of late capitalism . . . We wish to highlight the importance of and the possibilities offered by the ludic in disrupting the exercise of power, whatever its intent.

Arguments are often presented as battles, but fighting is not the only way to engage with others. As I emphasized in Chapter 4, the development of postmodern ideas has happened through and by the development of politically radical theories from the perspectives of feminism, black studies and theories of social class. There are plenty of educational researchers who work across the apparent division between metaphysics and postmodernism (Davies 1989; Walkerdine 1990; Lather 1991; Rattansi 1992; Weiner 1994; Haw 1996; Sewell 1996a). Indeed, all the researchers whose work is the subject of my examples of social justice research in Chapter 2 operate from time to time on both sides of the so-called battle lines (though not all of them do so in these particular pieces of research). These researchers were chosen as being different from each other: they do not all use the same theoretical stance. Some draw more from situated perspectives, some from textual deconstruction, some from analyses of micro circulations of power.[10] But, like Soper, we growl with the metaphysicians while we dance with the ironists. As dancers, we can see that the metaphysicians are moving in dances of their own. Rather like the fool in a morris dance, we move from growling and flailing alongside the dancers to playfully trying out new dance steps, weaving between, beside and around the metaphysicians. It is part of the game to dance around the metaphysicians, even while we dodge their blows and skip out of the way. But the fool's dancing depends on there being growls and flails to play with, and gets its point from them.

How did battle lines get drawn up in such a misleading fashion? One answer is that the situation is very complex, so it has been necessary for various authors to present it in simplified terms. (I think this is unavoidable. There are plenty of examples of it in this book, after all.) The danger of such presentations is that they come to be believed, and recirculated, as the complete picture, when in fact they are only particular, simplified versions of it. This seems to be what has happened in the case of the supposed disagreements between 'postmodernists' and theory related to social justice. Some of the former have problems with some of the latter. This does not mean there is a generalized problem. This can be shown by taking a closer look at particular examples of supposed disagreement. It can be seen quite quickly that the disagreement is less a case of a single, fixed, clear boundary which divides opposing camps than of shifting boundaries marking alliances formed for particular purposes between those holding views which only rarely fit into pigeonholes labelled, for instance, 'postmodern', 'humanist', 'positivist' or 'rational-technical'. For example, while scientific–rational–progress can be contrasted with power–knowledge–resistance (e.g. Foucault), it can equally well be contrasted with jouissance–play–deconstruction (e.g. Derrida) or pagan–libidinous (e.g. Lyotard). High theorists of the so-called 'postmodern' include (often in the teeth of their own disavowal of the term 'postmodern') Lyotard, Derrida, Irigaray, Foucault and Kristeva. These are not theorists who agree with each other, to put it mildly. (Others, slightly less canonical, but highly regarded as leading the field, and often equally nervous of the label 'postmodern', include Flax, Gilroy, Hall, Haraway and Said. Again, their collective work could not be said to constitute a theory, or even a school.)[11] Similarly, in one of the camps often opposed to postmodernism, the liberals, it is hard to know just who counts as 'liberal'. Walzer, for instance, appears with Taylor as a critic of liberalism in Sandel's (1984) collection. However, on the back of his *Spheres of Justice*, Daniel Bell hails the book as 'the foundation of a new, emergent liberalism'.

We can usefully look at the Enlightenment project itself, so often said to be antithetical to postmodernism. It is true that it can be understood as a grand narrative of progress, in which each generation builds on the advances of the one before, using reason to help them. This is indeed how John Gray describes it. He says that the Enlightenment project is 'universal emancipation', and aspects of the Enlightenment include: 'its assault on cultural difference, its embodiment of Western cultural imperialism as the project of a universal civilisation, and its humanist conception of humankind's relations with the natural world' (Gray 1995: viii). Further, it can be said that this is to be achieved through scientific and technical means. Even further, such rationalism, science and technical expertise can be said to be part of the liberal view of humanity as rational, social atoms forming social contracts with each other in order to realize their individual ends. But that the Enlightenment is claimed by such liberal-humanists as their own does not mean that this is the only possible interpretation; or even that those who hold some of these liberal interpretations need hold them all.[12]

The Enlightenment can also be taken as being primarily about constructing a critique *using* reason, which, logically but paradoxically, includes the critique *of* reason by reason. In this view, one of the central tenets of the Enlightenment is that criticality and reason, within the limits of reason, are the grounds of understanding. Another of the central tenets of the Enlightenment is optimism about actions for improvement. This may be a guarded optimism, but anyway it is a kind of optimism. I take each point in turn; I look first at critique and then at possibilities of improvement.

In Foucault's (1984) article on the Enlightenment, he suggests that in his article called 'What is Enlightenment', Kant caught the main characteristics of what Foucault calls modernity. That is, modernity is not to be defined in temporal terms (i.e. as of a particular historical time) but in terms of an attitude, or 'a mode of relating to contemporary reality' (*ibid*.: 39). This, argues Foucault, is an attitude of critique:

Kant in fact describes Enlightenment as the moment when humanity is going to put its own reason to use, without subjecting itself to any authority; now it is precisely at this moment that critique is necessary, since its role is that of defining the conditions under which the use of reason is legitimate in order to determine what can be known, what must be done, and what may be hoped.

(*ibid.*: 38)

This attitude of critique is something Foucault claims in his own work, and he also uses it against the too easy equation of Enlightenment with any one philosophical, political or practical system of modern times. In particular, 'This permanent critique of ourselves has to avoid the always too facile confusions between humanism and Enlightenment' (*ibid.*: 43).

Foucault's argument is not an isolated or an idiosyncratic view. Hutchings shows this in her intricately argued, careful study of Kant's continuing political relevance for all shades of current political thought (Hutchings 1995). She traces the influence of Kantian critique on the very different political positions of the influential modern political theorists, Habermas, Arendt, Foucault and Lyotard – the first two of whom are *not* postmodern by any stretch of a criterion.[13] Hutchings analyses the inherent instability of critique, showing how it is precisely this instability which is so productive of useful analyses, at the same time as it undermines all possible analyses. She demonstrates how Kant's analysis is one in which:

critique sets itself tasks which it is unable to fulfil. The dual determination of critique in the acknowledgement of reason's limitations and the assertion of its legislative power implies a set of dichotomies and a series of attempts to overcome them. This opens up Kant's texts to opposing interpretations and enables him to be read . . . along both liberal and authoritarian lines.

(Hutchings 1996: 37)

She points out that this productivity and instability apply to knowledge, politics and morals. As a result of this critique, something which is a defining feature of the Enlightenment, and so of contemporary Western thought, the domains of knowledge and value are inherently insecure.

The possibilities of improvement hinge on the possibility of acting on common values and understandings, uncertain as they are. However, this possibility does not depend on there being only one interpretation of the Enlightenment, any more than do any other outcomes of critique. This argument is coherent with those turns in postmodern thought which express a guarded optimism that is not the utopian thinking of meta-narrative. This is not an optimism about overall and continuing improvement in a system as a whole – the ideals of rational-scientific improvement. Rather, it is an optimism that it is worth struggling for justice, knowledge and understanding, while accepting that there will be no final victory. Both Lyotard and Foucault have this kind of guarded optimism (which Foucault calls pessimism). In an interview, Foucault comments on the ethics and politics underlying his theories:

> My point is not that everything is bad, but that everything is dangerous, which is not exactly the same as bad. If everything is dangerous, then we always have something to do. So my position leads not to apathy but to a hyper- and pessimistic activism.
>
> I think the ethico-political choice we have to make every day is to determine which is the main danger.
>
> (Foucault 1984: 343)

In another interview, he says in relation to education:

> Power is not an evil. Power is strategic games . . . Let us also take something that has been the object of criticism, often justified: the pedagogical institution. I don't see where the evil is in the practice of someone who in a given game of truth, knowing more than another, tells him what he must do, teaches him, transmits knowledge to him, communicates skills to him. The problem is rather to know how you are to avoid in these practices . . . the effects of domination.
>
> (Foucault 1988: 18)

Lyotard finishes his book *The Postmodern Condition* with an 'outline of a politics that would respect both the desire for justice and the desire for the unknown.'

> Social pragmatics does not have the 'simplicity' of scientific pragmatics. It is a monster formed by the interweaving of various networks of heteromorphous classes of utterances (denotative, prescriptive, performative, technical, evaluative, etc.) . . .
>
> Consensus has become an outmoded and suspect value. But justice as a value is neither outmoded nor suspect. We must thus arrive at an idea and practice of justice that is not linked to that of consensus . . .
>
> A recognition of the heteromorphous nature of language games is a first step in that direction. This obviously implies a renunciation of terror, which assumes that they are isomorphic and tries to make them so.
>
> (Lyotard 1984: 65–6)

Not surprisingly, such a guarded optimism is also to be found in the growling, flailing, dancing, laser-wielding ludic metaphysicians of anti-racist, feminist, class-based educational research. They present a space for ethics, but not for any universal-rational ethics. It is an optimism that could also be called pessimism, since there is no hope of a final success; an optimism that the struggle is worthwhile anyway.

One of the clearest arguments for what he calls postmodern ethics is put by Zygmunt Bauman. He argues that morality has no need of rational foundations and hard and fast principles. On the contrary, he says, the rationalization and the principles are abstractions from everyday life, which is, always and inevitably, moral. What is more, the lack of any hard and fast system for deciding moral questions only reflects the situation that 'moral choices are indeed choices' and not the 'rectifiable effects of human weakness, ignorance or blunders' (Bauman 1993: 32). He goes on:

> Human reality is messy and ambiguous – and so moral decisions, unlike abstract ethical principles, are ambivalent. It is in this sort of world that we must live; and yet, as if defying the worried philosophers who cannot conceive of an 'unprincipled' morality, a morality without foundations, we demonstrate day by day that we can live, or learn to live, or manage to live in such a world, though few of us would be ready to spell out, if asked, what the principles that guide us are.

This is an ethics that emphasizes that people have a limited agency in making decisions in local rather than universal circumstances. It promises no more and no less than a continuing struggle in a non-determined social world. This is not a recipe for paralysis or apathy, as Foucault commented above. In the context of education, Gore (1993: xv) comments that for her, as a teacher:

> Perhaps it is in postmodern times that one can rest with the ongoing struggles of an endeavor that will never reach conclusion, that will never arrive at a final solution. I certainly find my ongoing struggle for pedagogies enabling in comparison with the failure inherent in the modernist framing of its own enterprise.

Or, as Robin Richardson (1996: 36) puts it:

> We haven't lost yet and we're never going to lose, because for ever the story is going to be continued. True, we're never, for the same reason, going to win, either. But that's a small price to pay – isn't it? – for never losing. Let me praise headteachers whose schools are full of unfinished stories, and of stories which are so good and strong that the children and teachers go back to them time and again, repeating, rehearsing, finding new facets in the familiar, exploring new depths in the already known. A story is unfinished not by virtue of ending in mid-air, not by teasing to an anti-climax, but by leaving layer on layer to be still unwrapped, and by inviting therefore repetition and return.

Richardson refers to narrative and to the exhilarating lack of closure inherent in it. This view is taken up in the suggestion that postmodern educational research tells a different kind of story from the ones we have become used to in standard, modernist research. It is usual to tell stories where problems are resolved and in which the researcher overcomes any obstacles. Critics point out that these are a kind of hero story, stories of triumph and redemption. It is suggested that in the place of these hero stories should be layered and multiple stories, which include those stories of ruin that accompany and shadow the stories of triumph in standard research reports (Stronach and MacLure 1997).

In spite of all the claims to the contrary, I have argued that postmodernism is hospitable to the holding of values in research, and is therefore relevant to the project of trying to improve the education of children and students. However, I must acknowledge that a view of postmodernism as 'anything goes' relativism, and of conservative, ludic politics, retains a strong hold. Further, of course, the debate is still very much alive for educational researchers. Chapter 1 of Stronach and MacLure's (1997) book on postmodern research is a useful introduction to this question, and, unusually for introductory discussions, remains within the idiom of postmodern deconstruction and layered reporting.

There are implications for educational researchers about how to go forward with research for social justice. For me, what has come to be called postmodern thinking (much of it derived directly from feminist theory, in my case) has been helpful and influential, as can be seen in the kinds of methodology that frame the social justice project described in Chapter 2. This influence can be summarized as follows. First, the view that educational research is part of practice means that discourse has to be understood in terms of power as well as in terms of description. Second, the influence of postmodern thinking can be found in the emphasis on situated perspectives and specific context, including the micro-context. Third, it is very helpful to lose undue optimism about the possibilities of finding any utopian solution, or of finding a framework which will explain everything for once and for all. It is more helpful to realize that any solution is provisional and revisable in the light of critique.

Those of us researching for justice, and finding ourselves helped by what can be called postmodernism, can continue to go ahead. But it is a slow, careful process in which we find ourselves picking our way very carefully through the difficult terrain. This is not like the grand motorway of a metanarrative. On the contrary, it is a journey in which we need to pick our way, paying attention as we go to how we change the landscape by inhabiting it. We also need to note that people have tried to drive motorways of metanarrative across it. Our journeys have to take account of them and of the traffic on them: traffic we have to negotiate as it alternatively races ahead or slams on the brakes. Sometimes, it does this right across our paths, because the motorways, like our slower paths, form a feature of the landscape as we move carefully on.

Uncertain ways of knowing

I now turn to the question of uncertain knowledge and how to get it. I present an outline theory of uncertain knowledge, for the purposes of educational research. It is one thing to claim that values are local or provisional. It is quite another to make similar claims about knowledge. A relativism about knowledge is often regarded as more dangerous than one about values. However, the Enlightenment critique applies as much to what can be *known* as it does to what *should be done*.

My arguments over the last few chapters have brought me to the position to discuss uncertain knowledge. In Chapter 3, I discussed the way in which agency constrained what could be known about human beings, partly because of the unavoidability of interpretation and partly because the investigation of those interpretations raised ethical issues. In Chapter 4, I took this further, by discussing facts and values and how far they might be separable. In doing so, I drew on the empirical tradition in the person of David Hume. The discussions were about the processes involved in making sense of data. It was argued that looking for patterns and making judgements about their significance is a process which is affected by the values of the person who is doing it. The process is, itself, part of the production of knowledge. Thus, the values and politics behind the process become part of the knowledge. It was argued that such interpretations coalesced into 'regimes of truth' as a result of the circulations of power in a society.

Thus, as the argument has progressed, Hume's simple distinction between fact and value has been eroded. On the one hand, the idea of a 'value' has lost its Humean clarity in social structures and the workings of power. On the other, as discussions progressed, the idea of a simple fact seemed to be losing its application. Or, rather, as a result of the discussion of interpretations of states of affairs, perspectival knowledge and regimes of truth, it became less important: a fact was only one part of what is called 'knowledge'. A look at research – whether as the discovery, construction or (re)presentation of knowledge – shows that there does indeed seem to be an extraordinary range in what is counted as knowledge, including information, concepts, skills (widely understood) and personal perspectives. In the first section of this chapter I listed some kinds of research which demonstrate this. However, it could be argued that some of this 'research' does not produce 'knowledge' at all, properly speaking, but rather 'scholarly activity' or 'scholarship' (Siraj-Blatchford and Siraj-Blatchford 1997). Before going on to present an outline theory of uncertain knowledge, I set the discussion in context by outlining some of the broad contours of the wider debate about the nature of knowledge.[14]

Various dichotomies and taxonomies have been suggested in answer to the question 'What is knowledge?' One particularly influential distinction is the one drawn between knowledge which is rational (gained from reason) and knowledge which is empirical (gained from data). Both of these are often supposed to lead to certainty, in their different ways, although there is a long tradition of scepticism in both cases. Another well known and useful distinction is between 'knowledge that' (so called factual or propositional knowledge) and 'knowledge how to' (competencies, skills). Only the former is a candidate for certainty, because skills cannot be true or false. Both, however, can be uncertain in the sense that they are fallible, that they can be revised and worked on in order to make them better. This distinction is closely related to the one drawn between theory and practice, since there it is arguable that theory, like 'knowledge that', is independent of an individual knower (even where it bears the marks of who formulated it), although practice, like 'knowledge how to', has to be carried out by a particular individual.

There are further, related, distinctions which are useful for those people interested in doing educational research in conditions of uncertainty and diversity. There are those put forward by Lyotard in his report on the state of knowledge in an age of global communication, *The Postmodern Condition*. He argues for a distinction between knowledge which can be commodified and a range of other kinds of knowledge. Knowledge which can be commodified is either 'information', which can be expressed in bytes of information, or 'competence', which can be measured against the yardstick of efficiency. Other kinds of knowledge are those which are organized around language games not only of truth and of efficiency but also of ethical wisdom (justice and/or happiness) and beauty (auditory and visual sensibility). Foucault, as I said in Chapter 4, talks of regimes of truth. He also talks (Foucault 1980: 82) of 'subjugated knowledges', which are 'particular, local, regional knowledges' ('such as that of a psychiatric patient, ill person, nurse and doctor, parallel and marginal as they are to the knowledge of medicine') in relation to the formal systemization of those knowledges further up the hierarchy. Patricia Hill Collins, writing from the perspective of black feminist thought, uses the term 'subjugated knowledges' to refer to music, literatures, daily conversations and everyday behaviour (Collins 1990: 202). Haraway, as I said in Chapter 4, talks of 'situated knowledges', differentiated by the communities of knowers from which they come. Rose argues for responsible knowledge shaped by love and care, rather than denying both (Rose 1994).[15] Implicit in the distinctions drawn above is an underlying theme related to who constructs the knowledge and who decides if it is reliable. This is something I come back to in Part III, where I discuss questions of reliability and validity.

My outline theory of uncertain knowledge is a general epistemological position which can be formulated as a result of the arguments of this chapter. It takes into account the range of knowledge for different purposes: different language games, different audiences, different positions in relation to power. It also depends on the (Enlightenment) view that any epistemology is formulated in conditions of critique. This applies to practical knowledge and to wisdom as much as to propositional, factual knowledge. Since this is a general position, it overarches the differences between the epistemologies discussed, but it does not deny the significance of the differences. For there are serious differences, with real consequences for educational research. I describe the position as an 'outline' to draw attention to the fact that it only needs to be detailed enough for the purposes for which it is needed. It will not resolve all epistemological problems! It is, however, enough to provide a framework for the next chapter, where I put forward some principles for educational research for social justice.

The outline position is as follows: the best that can be done is to look for knowledge from different perspectives, in the context of the social and historical situations in which it was discovered, interpreted and constructed. This knowledge is thus self-consciously situated in its context, and always subject to revision. There are three important consequences for researchers.

First, there is no possibility of the acquisition or creation of stable, unchanging knowledge, since all knowledge must be subject to critique from other viewpoints, which may fundamentally revise current structures. The construction of knowledge is as much a process of reform as of revolution, as much revolution as reform. New theory uses old theory as a springboard, the difference being that it is less narrow in its perspectives. The various reconfigurations affect other structures, so it is necessary for there to be a continual questioning of the new political alignments being found. Thus there is no stable, unchanging state of knowledge; so even while some old narrowness of perspective is lost, inevitably some new problems of narrowness will be created. This is not the smooth progress hoped for under positivism. To turn again to metaphor, it is not like building a better nuclear bunker, intended to last under all possible attacks. On the other hand, nor is it like building a house of cards, liable to come crashing down at the slightest challenge. It is more like building a garden, where work never stops and where unexpected growth can alter the development of the whole.

Second, since knowledge bears the marks of its knowers, attention must be paid to how it is grounded in the individual perspectives and positions in a discourse of the researcher and the subjects. The 'individual' is understood here to be part of many communities, which are describable in terms of perspectives and positionings, such as 'teacher', 'child', 'adult', 'student', 'gay', 'bisexual', 'heterosexual', 'Muslim', 'Hindu', 'Christian', 'Catholic', 'Protestant' and so on and on. It would be impossible to pin down any one individual with an exhaustive description of the many ways of working of power and values at these micro and macro levels. Yet some or many of them are likely to be relevant for the construction of knowledge. It is, at the least, important not to allow the norm for all knowledge to be set using the perspective of white, middle-class, Protestant, straight, able-bodied males.

Third, it is not just perspective and position that need to be taken into account, but also the particular ethical and political views of the researcher. These cannot be simply read off his or her position – and could not be, even if it were completely specifiable. Individuals are never determined by their positions, even though they are constrained by them, as I have argued elsewhere (Griffiths, 1995a). The ethical and political views underlying the getting of knowledge should be as clear as possible, even while accepting that absolute clarity is an impossibility, since they cannot be fully specified.[16] The argument of this book has been that acknowledging ethical and political views helps both to unmask any bias that is implicit in those views, and also to provide a way of weighing up the validity of the knowledge.

At the beginning of this chapter, I said that I would move from leaning to one side of the fence, to jumping down from it. I have now done that, in respect of the nature of educational research, of the use of values as a guide in research and of the search for uncertain knowledge. To summarize: (a) educational research is for the improvement of the education of children and students; (b) what constitutes that improvement is always uncertain, and will remain so; (c) however, it is worthwhile struggling for justice and knowledge, even though they remain fallible and uncertain. This can be construed as a pessimistic optimism, especially as the hope of really useful, certain knowledge or of agreed and certain knowledge diminishes and fades with each new setback in trying to gain it. It gives us a principled though uncertain way to go on. In the next chapter, I relate this to the particular case of social justice in educational research.

Notes

1 As I explain in this section, this is not quite the same as 'research in educational settings', as in the title of this series.

2 See Chapter 6, note 6.

3 This is *as well as* the consideration of value and politics in any research related to human beings, the position which I argued for in Chapter 4. In the context of a university, a logical consequence of this position is a demarcation between kinds of research which might be appropriate in different departments of the university, even where there is a considerable overlap of interest. Some departments, like education (and also like medicine, nursing, town planning, applied social sciences and civil engineering), seek to improve an area of human life, and so must be focused on the application of their research. Others, like history, philosophy, psychology, sociology or physics, need not be. For departments focused on improvement, the application of research can be fairly distant, but it must be there in the long run. Some departments, like education (but also like applied social science and town planning), are necessarily about enhancing the conditions in which people live their lives.

4 This is a plea for tolerance against inappropriate dreams of purity, and against, therefore, the kind of methodological and epistemological cleansing that various

factions (including action researchers, positivist-inclined empiricists, ethnographers and philosophers) have called for in relation to others.

5 See Cordingly (1996), Foster and Hammersley (1996), Hargreaves (1996, 1997), Whitehead (1996), Gray *et al.* (1997) and Hammersley (1997). See also Ranson (1996) for an overview of various public arenas.

6 Included here is Lyotard himself. See, for instance, the article in *Philosophy Explained to Children*: 'Notes on the meaning of "post-" ' (Lyotard 1992).

7 In what follows, I am attempting to draw a map of a range of difficult theory relevant to the argument here. While some educational researchers will want to follow up some of this, others will have neither the time nor the inclination to follow this intricate, many-sided debate for themselves. I am aiming to be of use to both sets.

8 I've done some growling myself in my time, including in an article in which, like Soper in her article, I end up doing some dancing too (Griffiths 1995b).

9 'Ludic' postmodernism is self-consciously playful with words and ideas, as Usher and Edwards are not. Since they are so serious, it is easy to quote like this. But the far more ludic work of Stronach (1997), and Stronach and MacLure (1997), while less quotable, is a convincing exemplar of Usher and Edwards's argument.

10 'Situated perspectives', 'textual deconstruction' and 'micro circulations of power' are terms referring to particular frameworks of particular theorists: Haraway, Derrida and Foucault, respectively.

11 I include reference to all these many theorists partly to help those readers who are familiar with this work to orientate themselves in relation to my arguments. This is an attempt at inclusion. Readers who have not met any of these theorists need not feel excluded: they can simply read past.

12 Not even all physical scientists do. See the series of reflections on the issues of science, politics and positivism by the eminent physicist, Werner Heisenberg (1971).

13 These are all well known in political theory, and in some circles of educational research too. See note 11, above.

14 Lest it be thought I am doing this: I am making no attempt to outline 2000 years and more in the history of epistemology, much of which has been an attempt to answer the questions: What can we know? What is knowledge?

15 I could go on for some time without being exhaustive. There are other very useful ones which have commonalities and continuities with what has already been alluded to. Particularly well known conceptions include dialogical knowledge and personal knowledge, both of which are influential in the field of action research.

16 The quotation from Taylor in Chapter 4 makes a related point about self-interpretations, and how they could never come to a final closure.

6 | Educational research for social justice: a framework

Defining and understanding social justice

In this chapter, even more than Chapter 5, I 'get off the fence', taking a position on the nature of social justice and on educational research for social justice. In the book as a whole, I have been drawing on my own research and practice over a decade and more (as I explained in Chapter 1). In all that research I was indebted to others for their help and ideas – whether it could be called 'joint' research or not. However, this chapter is very much the product of collaborative research, the research into social justice that I described in Chapter 2. In particular, the next section is the result of collaboration in that research project, and I need to acknowledge my co-researchers and give due weight to the contribution of the rest of the group who made it – who are continuing to make it. I say 'continuing to make' because the version used in this book is a snapshot of a developing process. The use I make of the project is my responsibility, but I am not the sole author of it. That is, it arose as a result of collaboration, but not all the participants would agree with all that I say about it, or the use I make of it.[1]

I have not yet explained in any detail what I mean by social justice. Instead, I have worked from examples and relied on the common understandings of the term to be clear enough for my purposes. In addition, in Chapter 1 (pages 12–13), I stated three principles of social justice, very briefly. The time has come to look at the idea more directly. First, I look at my choice of the term 'social justice'. Why do I not, for instance, talk about 'equality issues' or 'equal opportunities'? Or, indeed, why do I not avoid these terms by being specific and naming the particular source of injustice, using terms like feminism, anti-racism, social class, sexuality or some combinations of these (like Patricia Hill Collins's 'black feminist')? Why do I prefer to work with the term 'social justice', a term which has not been as widely used as 'equal opportunities', 'feminism' or 'anti-racism'?

One reason for choosing the term 'social justice' is precisely because it has been less used. As a result, it has not (yet) suffered the kind of attack as a term that the more well known terms have. The attack on terms which have gained currency as a result of equal opportunities movements has been very successful in altering the rhetoric – the discourse – of the debate. It has been based on using the notion of 'political correctness' – as if being 'correct' was a wrong thing to be. Patricia Williams, an American lawyer, describes this as rhetorical robbery:

> The roadblock that the moral inheritance of the civil rights movement has encountered in the attack on 'political correctness' strikes me as just such rhetorical robbery – it is a calculated devaluation of political property values not less than the 'white flight' organized by the National Association of Realtors a few decades ago, which left us with the legacy of the 'inner city'.
>
> (Williams 1995: 28)

The struggle is not over. Terms like 'equality' or 'equal opportunities' may be claimed back at a later date. For now, their devaluation is a reality that needs to be acknowledged.

Another reason for choosing the term is that 'social justice' is a broader term than 'equality'. There are plenty of times when strict equality would be waived for reasons of social justice. In education, the diversion of resources to children who have special needs is widely agreed to be just, whether or not it can be described in terms of formal equality. Few classroom teachers would advocate that resources or time should be distributed between children on the basis of strict equality. The converse does not hold. The claims of social justice are not waived for reasons of equality. Social justice is more fundamental than equality as a guide to how we should act in relation to society and its educational institutions. The history of the terms is relevant to these arguments.

There has been a considerable general movement (with varying successes) over the past five decades and more for a fairer, less oppressive society. In Chapter 1 (pages 9–12), I gave a brief account of the historical context of the search for social justice in education. This has been a movement towards opening up, from the few to the many, chances of personal fulfilment, and of finding the rewards, prizes and enjoyments of living in society. All of these include schooling. Over the years, the focus has changed from a movement predominantly focused on social class to one where race and gender issues are more prominent.

Over that time, the movement in Britain has been identifiable by the use of a number of terms. Prominent among these have been 'equality' and 'equal'. The use of the term 'equal opportunities' has generated some problems. Some of these are well known philosophical difficulties with the idea of equality, well expressed by Bernard Williams in his classic article, 'The idea of equality':

It has only too often been pointed out that to say that all men are equal in all those characteristics in respect of which it makes sense to say that men are equal or unequal, is a patent falsehood . . . Faced with this obvious objection the defender of the claim is likely to offer a weaker interpretation . . . it is their common humanity which constitutes their equality . . . If all the statement does is to remind us that men are men it does not do very much . . . A similar discomfiture tends to overcome the practical maxim of equality. It cannot be the aim of this maxim that all men should be treated alike in all circumstances or even that they should be treated alike as much as possible.

(Williams 1973: 230–1)

Other difficulties were noticed by E. P. Thompson as long ago as 1961. He pointed out that the rhetoric of 'equal opportunities' was politically ambiguous, and, moreover, had the effect of making it difficult to articulate a broader vision of equality.

'Get on, get ahead, get up!' say the advertisers. 'The Opportunity State', says the Conservative Party, 'Equality of Opportunity', says the official Labour Party echo. In this orchestration of competitive values, how is incipient heresy to be heard at all? To say that our aim should be, not equality of opportunity within an acquisitive society, but a society of equals; that we need, not more ladders, but, more generous patterns of community life; to say these things is simply to proclaim one's political irrelevance.

(Thompson 1980: 2)

The accuracy of Thompson's criticism has been confirmed by the use that has been made of the rhetoric of equal opportunities in the decades since he wrote.

Between them, Thompson and Williams pointed to the way the concept of equality was to be politically neutralized. In the decades since they wrote, equality has been treated either as part of a discourse of sameness (with the implication that it is evidently wrong or evidently dreary) or as part of a discourse of competition. Thus, there has been a move to *deride* aspirations for equality – for instance, as the politics of envy (Ball 1990; Myers 1990) – while simultaneously *containing* such aspirations by identifying equality with equal competition in a market place governed by economic liberalism: 'Equality to be unequal', as Margaret Thatcher memorably put it. Happily, it is true, as Cynthia Cockburn (1991) points out, that ambiguity in the meanings attached to 'equal opportunities' can be played on in order to generate coalitions between radicals, liberals and conservatives to benefit disadvantaged groups in a way that escapes identifying equality as either 'sameness' or 'the market'.[2]

For all these reasons, there is a growing preference for using a new term which captures much of the same set of issues. The phrase 'social justice' is reasserting itself as one of the most useful terms to use. It is allied in meaning to 'equality', but has not (yet) suffered similar political attacks. It does, of course, lay itself open to political attacks, as all terms do. The users of terms have to guard against further 'rhetorical robbery', as the American lawyer, Patricia Williams, herself black, describes it (see page 86). As she says,

> The rapid obsolescence of words even as they drop from our mouths is an increasingly isolating phenomenon. In fact it feels like a form of verbal blockbusting. I move into a large meaningful space, with great connotations on a high floor with lots of windows, and suddenly all the neighbours move out. My intellectual aerie becomes a known hangout for dealers in heresy and other soporific drugs, frequented by suspect profiles (if not actual suspects) and located on the edge of that known geological disaster area, the Slippery Slope.
>
> (Williams 1995: 27–8)

Social justice is an idea with a long history in philosophy and politics. It carries many of the same connotations as 'equality', but, as I have indicated, it does not cover quite the same set of meanings. The question of social justice was raised most influentially by Plato in *The Republic*. The question Socrates[3] posed was the possibility of working out a system which would ensure the good for the city-state and for its citizens. Plato's argument closely connects the questions of individual morality with public justice: the question of why individuals should be just, with the question of what a just city-state would be like. In Part VI, he reminds us: 'We were concerned . . . to ensure the highest degree of happiness for the community as a whole without concentrating attention on the happiness of any particular section of it.' This is still a useful place to start, even if his particular proposals for doing this are less attractive. There are few who would defend his division of the state into three, with the topmost division being the ruling philosopher kings. Happily, however, this is not a necessary conclusion from his starting point, because the conclusions also depend on his particular views of human nature and of community.

Aristotle's discussions of ethics and politics draw on Plato's, but they were developed both with and against him. They have also been immensely influential on Western thinking about social justice. In the *Politics*, he says: 'The good in the sphere of politics is justice, and justice consists in what tends to promote the common interest' (III, 11, 1282b14). Earlier he explains what he means by the common interest:

> People desire to live a social life even when they stand in no need of mutual succour; but they are also drawn together by a common interest, in proportion as each attains a share in the good life. The good life is the chief end, both for the community as a whole and for each of us individually.
>
> (III, 6, 1278b6)

In the *Politics*, Aristotle distinguishes between (social) justice and the law. Justice (i.e. social justice) includes the law, but goes beyond it (*Politics*, III, 11, 1282b). Justice is that which promotes the well-being of communities and of each of the individuals within them.[4]

Aristotle was particularly concerned with justice as the right distribution of benefits in a society ('distributive justice').[5] In the *Politics*, he cites his earlier conclusions in the *Nicomachean Ethics* (V, 5):

> Justice is that in virtue of which the just man is said to be a doer, by choice, of that which is just, and one who will distribute either between himself and another or between two others not so as to give more of what is desirable to himself and less to his neighbour (and conversely with what is harmful), but so as to give what is equal in accordance with proportion; and similarly in distributing between two other persons.

This identification of social justice with distributive justice has been extremely influential right up to the present time. In one of the most influential of recent accounts of social justice, Rawls says that the principles of social justice provide a way of assigning rights and duties, and distributing the benefits and burdens of social cooperation (Rawls 1972: 4). My own description, earlier in this section, of a movement towards a fairer, less oppressive society was as 'the opening up, from the few to the many, chances of personal fulfilment and the rewards, prizes and enjoyments of living in a society'; this is a kind of distributive justice. Education is central to it.

A working definition of social justice has emerged from this discussion:

1 It is the good for the common interest, where that is taken to include the good of each and also the good of all, in an acknowledgement that one depends on the other.
2 The good depends on there being a right distribution of benefits and responsibilities.

This is a definition which depends on ethical and other evaluations, since it depends on the interpretation of terms like 'good' and 'right'. It is, therefore, not a definition that can be applied mechanistically to a situation in order to generate an index of social justice. It has to be applied by human beings making evaluative judgements.

Given the centrality of ethical judgements, there is still plenty of room for interpretation and disagreement. Moreover, such interpretations of how to achieve justice also depend on views of human nature and of community. They also depend, as Aristotle himself pointed out, on what counts as 'equal in accordance with proportion', and this varies with different conceptions of society. He discussed Greek forms of government: kingship, oligarchy, democracy. David Miller, in his historical analysis of different conceptions of distributive justice held by a wider range of societies, comes up with three categories: the stable, hierarchical order; the solidaristic community; and the competitive market. All of these categories are still mirrored in educational communities. Moreover, a school is also embedded in its society, and so partakes of that society's characteristic conceptions of justice. He talks of the 'evaluative overtones' of any concept of justice, stating: 'To describe a state of affairs as just or democratic is to pass a favourable judgement on it' (Miller 1976: 7).

Although there may be only a limited agreement about justice, nobody is able to do without some conception of it.[6] Everybody makes evaluative judgements about the justice of communities and society. This is true even of those who deny that they do so. Libertarians like Hayek say that there is no such thing as social justice, only individuals following their own fortunes. My argument is similar to ones already made in earlier chapters about the inevitability of evaluations underpinning human actions. (See Chapter 4, especially pages 50–52, and the arguments made by Taylor and Midgley.) In the particular case of social justice, the Commission for Social Justice rightly points out that concepts like 'level playing field' are used by libertarians like Hayek as defining criteria of a just society (Commission for Social Justice 1993: 4). In recent years, educational managers, in common with managers from other areas, have sometimes denied that they are involved in anything evaluative: they claim that they are simply applying rational or scientific principles. This claim is false, as was persuasively argued by MacIntyre (1981) and by many others since. In the context of education, Padraig Hogan usefully analyses Murgatroyd and Morgan's book on total quality management and their claim to be untainted by ideology. He shows how, in fact, they promote a particular conception of education as 'a customer–supplier relationship, governed primarily by the competitive practices of a market economy' (Hogan 1995: 227).

As the surveys by Aristotle and Miller show, evaluative overtones change with time and place. What has attracted favourable judgements as 'just or democratic' in one historical set of circumstances has been very different from what has attracted the same judgements in other sets of circumstances. We need to develop our own judgements for our times. Miller's survey ended with the competitive market. Since he carried out his analysis, there has been an explosion in information technology and international communication and migration, leading to globalization and the diverse, plural, fast changing society we inhabit today. The perspectives of postmodernism have been developed to understand these circumstances. (What this means for value judgements has been discussed in more detail in the previous chapters, especially Chapter 5.) From these perspectives, there is no hope of finding a dominant perspective and meta-narrative of justice which will guide us, but, as explained in Chapter 5, we should be guided by justice, nevertheless. Justice is to be struggled for in particular circumstances, and understood in relation to them. What this means for educational research is the subject of the next section.

Defining and understanding social justice in educational research

In this section, I am in a position to answer one of the central questions of the book: the question of what an educational researcher for social justice is to *do*. I have answered some of the abstract questions underlying the actions of educational researchers for social justice. Now I am at the stage when I have built up a set of tools to use in constructing practice and I am able to look at those actions directly. These tools are:

1 A working definition of social justice in terms of the good of individuals and the complex society which they inhabit – and which inhabits them. This can be understood in terms of right distributions of benefits and responsibilities.
2 An approach to discovering, constructing, (re-)presenting and developing uncertain knowledge.
3 An affirmation of the significance of ethical principles, including of justice in developing that knowledge; an activism for fallible, risky, uncertain justice.

So far, the argument has been built up at a very abstract level, and only partly directed at education. However, the understandings that have been built up have dictated that the argument must remain very abstract in places, just as it is very concrete in others. The emphasis is on uncertainty, fallibility and risky judgements made in particular material, historical circumstances. Thus, the approach depends on it being made more concrete *only* in particular circumstances.

In other words, it is not an approach intended to provide a blueprint determining what goes on everywhere for all time.[7] I have been careful to talk of working definitions and critique. It is an approach which is dependent on ethical and political choices and judgements. Thus, however it is used, it is entirely revisable, and the judgements will never be closed and determinate. It is responsive to the particular perspectives of those involved at the time, or for whom this has relevance. For instance, feminism, antiracism, postcolonialism and similar movements are characterized by an attitude of being *for* women, black people or other disadvantaged social groups. (Compare the discussion of being *for* education and justice in Chapter 5, pages 71–9.) This is an attitude that does not give a *particular* politics, but it does require *some* politics. At the minimum, it means that the perspectives of women, black people and working-class people do not get overlooked in relation to gathering or using information. Nor do those of people with special needs and people whose sexuality is not straight heterosexual. It also means that the particular circumstances of educational research do not get lost in generalizations about the social sciences or the humanities.

I am talking, then, of social justice in education, and in educational research. In one sense, all educational research must be research for social justice, given my account of educational research and of social justice. I said that educational research is for improvements in education, with all the personal and political implications of that. This is a focus on social justice: on the good of the individual and the society of which she is a part. However, it is possible to make distinctions: some educational research is more directly focused on social justice, while some of it is at a further remove. Some of it is much more likely to achieve some improvement in social justice.

In Chapter 2, I distinguished some categories of research for social justice. These appear again here, slightly altered. There is an extra category of research where social justice implications are not acknowledged.

1 Research that is focused directly on particular injustices for categories of people: perspectives of particular groups, organized by gender, ethnicity, sexuality, social class; and also of groups such as children, teachers or others which seem to be at a relative disadvantage in the production of theory.
2 Research with a framework that depends on the researcher's orientation to justice issues, but which is 'about' something else.
3 Research with implications for social justice, in its implicit or explicit approach to educational improvement, but where this is ignored as an issue.
4 Research which has an approach to epistemology and methodology that is consistent with working for social justice.

This last category is very similar to the third category of Chapter 2. It was suggested there that epistemology or methodology was taken by some researchers to be a criterion to judge if a piece of research was for social justice. This new wording is less determinate. It points to something less prescriptive and more overarching than prescribing any one particular epistemology or methodology.

I can now offer some principles to guide an approach to educational research which are based on an approach to epistemology and methodology consistent with working for social justice. The principles are derived from my – our – research into social justice. The principles were formed through a process of iteration between philosophy and data, between theorizing and experience, between individual perspectives and joint constructions. They are the results of research: a kind of knowledge. The presentation of the research and its results is logical and schematic, rather than an historical narrative or a rigorous methodological account of their development. In short, they are presented as the result of an iterative process, but without a description of the actual processes of dialogue and adjustment.[8]

I claim these principles to be a kind of knowledge. Using the brief discussion of knowledge in Chapter 5, it can be seen that it is 'knowledge how' rather than 'knowledge that'. Further, it is based on evaluative language games rather than on marketable products. Moreover, as I have argued, knowledge is marked by its knowers. Like any other piece of knowledge, the set of principles is a result of a historically situated process by people inhabiting (and being inhabited by) particular social and material contexts. It is also the result of a series of attempts to revise it in the light of different perspectives. As I have argued, the development of the knowledge is a never-ending process. In its present state of development, the perspectives which have been brought to bear, while not being wholly specifiable, include, crucially, those of the people with whom I have worked most closely in developing it, especially my co-researchers in the social justice project. However, the process was begun before that, in my earlier work on justice in education. In particular, I want to draw attention to the following:

1 I came to working out the situation for educational research after having focused on schools.
2 I bring to my understanding of the situation my location in philosophy, especially feminist philosophy, as well as my location in educational research and practice.

It is now possible to show where the three broad principles in Chapter 1 (pages 12–13) came from. The approach is located in the three-fold view of knowledge described in Chapter 5, and also within ethical principles of social justice as described earlier in this chapter. These are put into the context of education (in Britain, in the late twentieth century). The question is always the practical one of what to do for the best, so it is not surprising that we came up with 'knowledge how' rather than 'knowledge that'.

First, there is no one right answer, although there are right ways of going about getting knowledge for social justice. All answers are revisable and subject to change as a result of critique. This idea was already present in earlier work (Griffiths and Davies 1995). It was amplified rather than overturned during the project, although my co-researchers were certainly not chosen for their agreement with such ideas. On the other hand, they were chosen to come from a great variety of educational contexts, and to have different values and political allegiances; at the same time, all of them were used to working in alliances for practical outcomes. This may have been influential in making this principle acceptable. As the project continued, the idea was developed into the view that each community and each generation involved in education (children, teachers, parents, lecturers, advisors, policy-makers) can remake their society (including that part of it which is education). In order to do this, they need *both* a sense of their own worth and significance, and also a sense of their responsibilities to each other and that society.

Second, justice is for individuals *and* for groups, neither of which can exist without the other. This is the view found in Plato and Aristotle. It is also found in discussions with educational practitioners, who have a concern both for the learning and well-being of the individual child, student or teacher, and for the learning and well-being of groups. These groups may be formed by the school (e.g. classes, streams, ages) or be defined in social terms (e.g. girls, boys, African-Caribbean children, council estate children, rural children, refugees, travellers). These are groups in which children present themselves in the institution of school, and which clearly contribute to their identity, and vice versa. Another way of expressing this is the affirmation of the importance of a rich, public life, in which all participate and which all create; and also of a rich private, personal life available for all. This is an affirmation of the personal and public nature of education. This perspective fits easily with the focus on the individual which is at the heart of British education, and also with the way schools are organized so that children get seen in groups.

Third, research for social justice has to take account of more consciously political groupings than the ones mentioned above. These include groups identified by their political concerns in relation to sexuality, feminism, racism and socialism. These categories are, clearly, related to the groups mentioned above, but with the difference that there is much more political consciousness and a concern with power and empowerment. I should not give the impression that these political groups are separate or separable. Rather, research for social justice has to take them into account in all the complexity of their cross-cutting and layering in interlocking, flexible boundaries. In Chapter 2, I explained how the social justice project dealt with this interlocking complexity. Between us we had a variety of political commitments, enabling us to avoid the twin traps of focusing on only one or two forms of injustice, to the exclusion of others, or of assuming that all of them were much the same.

Educational research for social justice

The project did not come up with definite proposals for items of 'good practice' in schools. Instead, it amplified the three basic principles into a more detailed set of revisable working principles for establishing better practice in particular schools. These were principles which could be followed by senior management teams of the kind that made up most of the project team. They can be seen in the Appendix.

The more detailed set of principles can be used, with some changes, for educational research, though with an important difference that educational research is wider than the school, which was the focus of the deputy heads and advisors of the project. They focused almost exclusively on social justice *in* the school, rather than social justice *from* the school, in relation to pupils' transitions to the world beyond. The principles for educational research, in contrast, apply both to social justice *in* educational research and to social justice *from* educational research.

1 *From* educational research: results of research should be good both for individuals and for society, with respect to social justice in and from schools.
2 *In* educational research: a learning educational research community by and for everyone in it and for everyone connected with it.

The principles have been constructed using the arguments given so far. In drafting them, for reasons of brevity, I use the term 'research', meaning 'research for social justice'. The principles are predicated on:

1 *An understanding of social justice.*
   1.1 Social justice is understood to be what is good for the common interest, where that is taken to include the good of each and the good of all, in an acknowledgement that one depends on the other.
   1.2 The good depends on there being a right distribution of benefits and responsibilities.
2 *An understanding of the purposes of educational research.*
   2.1 The purpose of educational research is to improve the education of children and students.
   2.2 Such improvement can be brought about by increased knowledge (including various kinds of knowledge, such as skills and understanding, as well as facts or propositions).
3 *An understanding of the epistemological context.*
   3.1 There is a requirement to take the interrelations of knowledge and power into account; including that the results of research can also be about *changes* in power.
   3.2 There is a requirement to pay attention to individuals and the variety of communities they inhabit (and which inhabit them).
   3.3 *All* the principles may always be the subject of critique and revisability.
   3.4 Openness, critique and revisability do not mean merely going along with the views of others. On the contrary, they mean re-evaluating the judgements of the researcher (or research team) in the light of those views, and then acting on them, even if the re-evaluation is unwelcome to those consulted.

The principles are as follows.

1 Improvement
A main reason for doing the research is to get improvement in social justice in and from education. Results of research include knowledge (but not only propositional knowledge or information) and improvements.

2 *Knowledge and learning*
A main reason for doing the research is to get knowledge and to learn from it. This is inclusive of various kinds of knowledge. It implies the best possible of whatever kind is aimed at.

3 *Radical change of any of the beliefs and values is possible*
Improvements and knowledge are always uncertain, so researchers must be prepared to change their minds radically, and to challenge others during and after doing the research. Research results and processes may surprise and discomfort any or all of the members of the research community, and also other educational researchers.

4 *Collaboration and consultation with the immediate research community*
Researchers need to work collaboratively with people as part of the community carrying out the research. It is difficult to establish hard and fast boundaries to this research community. Creating, establishing and working with such a diverse research community requires that all sectors respect and work with each other in conditions of trust and safety, in the interests of improving education. It is acknowledged that the processes of consultation and change are going to result in conflict and people feeling exposed when putting their views on the line. Waiving trust and safety can be morally justified, but only in extreme conditions.

5 *Openness to a wider community*
Researchers need to be open to the viewpoints of all concerned with the research. This means not only those in (4) above, but also users of the research and anyone else to whom it is relevant, e.g. pupils, teachers, support staff, parents, LEA advisors, the neighbourhood, policy-makers and pressure groups. Strategies are needed to listen to quiet, less powerful, voices.

6 *Openness to political groupings and perspectives*
Researchers need to seek out and be open to the view points of socio-political groups. There are alliances to be made between groups of people on the basis of, for instance, class, race, gender, social class and sexuality. They cross-cut alliances between, for instance, teachers, advisors, children and parents. All these groups need acknowledgement, support and understanding. This is a source of the reflexivity mentioned in (7) and (8).

7 *Reflexivity about own position and interests*
Reflexivity is needed about the researchers' own socio-political position and interests. Argument, anger and risk are all part of the process. Some of the feelings of risk come about because such consultation requires the

researcher(s) to be open to reflexivity about their own position and interests.

8 *Reflexivity about own understanding and values*
Reflexivity is needed about the researchers' own understanding and values.
It is important that the researchers acknowledge their allegiance to beliefs, values and traditions. Their most dearly held knowledge and values may be based in these principles of research for social justice, but these too are revisable.

9 *Perfection in research is not to be found*
There is no hope of doing perfect research. Utopia does not exist. All research programmes have to be constructed on the run, and against a background of social and educational change. Time constraints and compromises are inevitable. By the time the best possible design, methods and forms of dissemination are found, the situation will most probably have changed. It follows that all research must be subject to critique. Good research still needs to improve. This may mean that there are areas in which a research programme is excellent, but some other things may be out of its control altogether.

10 *Taking responsibility as part of the wider educational research community*
Researchers must recognize their responsibilities related to being part of the community of educational researchers. Good research also requires researchers to be open to the community of educational and other researchers, in a process of reflexivity related to dangerous knowledge and power. Advances always come as a patchwork or ragbag. There can never be a tidy overarching rationale or masterplan for improving fairness. Danger has to be acknowledged. Vigilance is needed. On the other hand, advances need to be recognized and celebrated.

Notes

1 Acknowledgements are due to the hard work and commitment, as well as the strength of their contribution, of: Beryl Bennett, Max Biddulph, Carol Davies, Carolyn Goddard, June Hunter, David Martin, Syble Morgan, Prakash Ross, Jacky Smith, Nada Trikic and Sue Wallace. I am also grateful to Gwen Schaffer, who began with the group, but moved jobs during the project.
2 A rhetoric of sameness or of competition remains pervasive in discussions of equality. See, for instance, the articles by White (1994) and Norman (1995), which point up the relative power of this discourse in relation to other ones which are to be preferred. In this at least, they seem to be in agreement, though they disagree about whether the alternatives can properly be described as discourses of equality.

3 Socrates is the hero of Plato's dialogues, but it is generally accepted that he is used as a mouthpiece for Plato's philosophy.

4 In the *Politics* (Book VII, 1), Aristotle says: 'We must not regard a citizen as belonging just to himself: we must rather regard every citizen as belonging to the city, since each is a part of the city.' This can be read as privileging the community over the individual, especially if, as in some translations, the word 'just' is omitted. The view of social justice I am putting forward privileges neither the individual nor the community. I am grateful to Padraig Hogan for our illuminating discussions on this point.

5 In the *Nicomachean Ethics* (Book V, 2), he distinguishes 'distributive justice', manifested in 'distributions of honour or money or other things that fall to be divided', from rectificatory justice, 'which plays a rectifying part in transactions between man and man' and is the concern of the law.

6 In his inaugural lecture, Wilfred Carr (1997) points out that there seems to be decreasing agreement about what education is for or how it should be studied – but that we cannot do without it. Indeed, it is more urgent than ever to speak 'for' education.

7 Compare here Lyotard's strategic games and Foucauldian activism, mentioned in Chapter 5.

8 See Chapter 2, note 6.

Part III | Practical possibilities

Introduction to Part III

This chapter marks the beginning of Part III of this book. The title of the first Chapter in this Part (Chapter 7) is 'Getting started' and readers may well want to begin here, turning to the earlier chapters later on. Alternatively, they may want to turn first to the chapters dealing with empowerment, getting knowledge, or reflexivity. The book has been written to make it easy to read in the order which suits the individual reader. A book is bound by the publishers so that some chapters come before others, but it can be read in any order. The more theoretical part happens to come first, but it is only very rarely that theoretical issues need to be sorted and solved before research can get started. Nor is it desirable that either is treated as prior. I say more about the usual stages of research in Chapter 7.

There could be several reasons for readers wanting to read Part III before they read Part II. Perhaps they are beginners. Perhaps they think they find abstract theory too difficult, or boring – or simply have not yet seen its relevance. People doing research are very different in their attitudes to the abstractions found in books on research. For some of them it is precisely this that attracts them to research. Others just want to get on with doing their investigations and need to be convinced of the relevance of abstractions. Yet others have an interest, but they lack confidence in their ability to handle what seems, from the outside, to be off-puttingly difficult. Others love the brain-stretching involved, but need to be convinced that it is actually relevant to the job in hand.

The kind of language I use is somewhat different in Parts II and III. This is because the parts of the book focus on different spheres of activity in educational research. Some appear mundane (almost common sense) and some esoteric (difficult to explain to people not involved in research). Some are hands-on and busy, while others are reflective and considered. These spheres interlock: none of them survive by themselves very well. But each of them has a language – a characteristic vocabulary and a way of organizing discussions – which suits them. These different kinds of language of educational research can be understood by analogy with the languages of different spheres of educational practice: the language of staffrooms, of classrooms, and of the education correspondents of national newspapers – not to mention the language appropriate to parents, pressure groups, advisors, Ofsted inspectors and so on. These are all mutually translatable even if something gets lost in translation. But each sphere works best with the language specially developed for it. Part III uses the kinds of language needed to talk about the practical business of getting on with research, rather than about underlying theory (which was the subject of Part II).

Principles on which to base decisions and choices about research were developed in Part II. In this part of the book I show how these principles of educational research for social justice make a difference to what can be done in practice. The full version of the principles can be found in Chapter 6, together with an explanation of what social justice is. But for ease of reference I give a very much shortened version here, together with the working definition of social justice.

Social justice is: what is good for the common interest, where that is taken to include the good of each and also the good of all, in an acknowledgement that one depends on the other. The good depends on there being a right distribution of benefits and responsibilities.

The principles that underpin working for social justice in educational research are as follows:

1 A main reason for doing the research is to get improvement in social justice in and from education.
2 A main reason for doing the research is to get knowledge and to learn from it.
3 Improvements and knowledge are always uncertain, so researchers must be prepared to change their minds radically, and to challenge others during and after doing the research.
4 Researchers need to work collaboratively with people as part of the community carrying out the research.
5 Researchers need to be open to the viewpoints of all concerned with the research.
6 Researchers need to seek out and be open to the viewpoints of socio-political groups.
7 Reflexivity is needed about the researchers' own socio-political positions and interests.
8 Reflexivity is needed about the researchers' own understanding and values.
9 There is no hope of doing perfect research. Utopia does not exist.
10 Researchers must recognize their responsibilities related to being part of the community of educational researchers.

It is important to note that the ten principles are not independent of each other: they are interlocking and cannot be treated as 'pick-and-mix'. The earlier frame the later ones and the later explain the earlier ones. Thus they all apply at the same time, though of course different ones come to the fore depending on the circumstances.

The chapters of Part III do not go through the principles in the order in which they appear in the list. In Chapter 7, I look particularly at Principle 9 (There is no hope of doing perfect research), Principle 3 (The possibility of radical change as a result of the research) and Principle 4 (The need to work collaboratively). These are 'getting started' issues. The following two chapters focus on the first two principles. Chapter 8 discusses Principle 1 (Getting improvement in social justice) in terms of empowerment and voice. Chapter 9 discusses Principle 2 (Getting knowledge and learning from it) in terms familiar in discussions of research methods: bias, validity and insider research. Chapter 10, the last chapter, widens the scope to consider reflexivity, including reflexivity about the wider educational research community and its responsibilities; it draws on Principle 7 (Reflexivity about the researchers' own socio-political positioning), Principle 8 (Reflexivity about the researchers' own understanding and values) and Principle 10 (Responsibility as part of the community of educational researchers).

7 | Getting started: the research process

Principled beginnings

Research reports give a misleading picture of research: the business of getting started on a piece of research, carrying it out and getting it used. Like any other practical activity (teaching, for instance), doing research is not a smooth, linear path from beginning to end. This chapter looks at practical research and its characteristically uneven, stumbling, wavering progress. This is done from the perspectives of Chapter 6's principle 9 (there is no hope of doing perfect research), principle 3 (the possibility of radical change as a result of the research) and principle 4 (the need to work collaboratively), which are particularly salient for dealing with 'getting started' issues – whatever the eventual choices and decisions about exactly what is done and why. It is also done from the perspective of issues as they present themselves to researchers setting out on research. So first I focus on finding, or being given, a methodology and set of techniques for research: the whole process of literature review, data collection, analysing, writing, reporting and influencing practice. I go on to talk about working with people – collaboration and the ethics involved.

Getting started in educational research may be a matter of: having an issue to explore; a feeling that more knowledge is needed in some area; a chance to investigate an area which matters; a wish to study a crucial question; a desire to get to grips with a pressing practical problem. The focus is on *what* will be researched, with some attention to *how*. Sometimes, increasingly, getting started is a matter of having the opportunity to join a team which has already been set up to do some educational research – often as the result of an institution having successfully bid for some funding. In this case, both the 'what' and the 'how' will already have been decided, at least in outline. Mehreen Mirza's research falls into this category.

The 'what' and the 'how' are matters much discussed in books about doing research. These discussions (like mine in Part II) tend to go on as though decisions about what to research, and how to do it, were relatively independent of practical constraints. This is a one-sided story about the design of research. The 'what' is discussed in epistemological terms of what can be known: that is, the proper objects of research and what counts as knowledge (see Chapters 3 and 5). The 'how' is discussed in terms of methodologies and techniques for getting knowledge (see Chapters 3 and 4). Very little attention is paid to the effect of practical constraints on research design.

Practical constraints always have an impact on what is researched and how. Researchers need to find ways of operating within and through the constraints. The sheer range of practical influences and constraints which have an impact on the course of a piece of research become evident as research gets under way. The amount of time available, the resources that can be allocated and the degree of support that can be expected from colleagues and supervisors are all crucial. Other constraints may also appear. For some, the likelihood that a funding body will back the research has an effect on the ways in which they design research projects. For some, the possibility that a particular investigation will lead to an MEd or a PhD is something that researchers need to take into account. For everyone, research design will be profoundly affected by the time scale and the financial, statistical or secretarial resources available: there are significant and obvious differences, for example, between research carried out by a self-funded research student, and research funded by a government policy-making body. The research survey into the achievement of ethnic minority pupils carried out by David Gillborn and Caroline Gipps is an example of a piece of research that would probably not have been done without government funding – and which had its size and scope strongly influenced by the scale and source of the funding allocated. Finally, the possibilities of impact on policy, practice or theoretical advancement are affected by the requirements of the funders, the availability of outlets and the acceptability of the research to gatekeepers. In Chapter 2, I described some of the effects of the ESRC on the course of my social justice project. Such influences are inescapable. Taken together, they form a formidable set of constraints on how research is conducted. They are particularly important for those wishing to research something that is likely to challenge the status quo – like improving social justice. Anyone interested in social justice has to find ways of researching issues that are directly relevant to it, and to do so using methods which enhance it, within such constraints – sometimes even in spite of the stated aims of the research.

Constraints are important, but there is always room for manoeuvre. David Gillborn and Caroline Gipps (see page 15), Mehreen Mirza (see page 17) and I (see page 21) were not hemmed in by the constraints on our research designs. All of us can take responsibility for how the research turned out. The principles help by indicating what needs to be kept in mind when making decisions. A balance always needs to be struck between these principled decisions and compromises with the practical constraints. But compromise is not a confession of failure, because the principles are written on the basis that any resolution will be uncertain and imperfect (principles 3 and 9). They indicate a process of working towards justice, which includes noting compromises and reflecting on what might be done to deal with them at another time. This is a process which continues all through the research. Mehreen Mirza's article about the methodology of her research was written, precisely, as part of such a process.

Different stages of research

Once the research has got started a researcher may have a relatively free hand to determine its course, or alternatively the directions of the project may be set by other members of the research team (the research director, for instance) or by outside funders. Whichever of these is the case, there is a logical framework of questions that each researcher (and research team) needs to address, and continue to address throughout. Issues of social justice are relevant to each of these questions.

1 What is worth researching?
2 What can be found out that is relevant?
3 How do I do that?
4 Is that really going to tell me what I want to know?
5 Does that realize the values underpinning approaches to question 1?

Question 1 concerns values and politics; questions 2 and 3 are epistemological. The last two questions bring together the issues of values and knowledge. Questions of value and epistemology precede questions of methodology and method, both of which precede evaluative questions about the use of the research.

The questions as I have presented them point to a logical framework which underpins the familiar set of stages of research as set out in research proposals and reports. They also show how social justice structures the whole framework from the beginning: it is not added on afterwards. This familiar set of stages starts with a question, and proceeds to: assessing the state of knowledge (often a literature review or, as in some action research, a personal position statement); deciding how to gather more knowledge (methodology); gathering evidence (results, sometimes including the researcher's own reasoning, actions and feelings); and using evidence to improve the state of knowledge (analysis and conclusions, including any personal or practical knowledge); and finally writing up, reporting, publicizing and acting on the relevant parts where appropriate.

There are two ways of viewing this logical framework: two threads which can be followed. First, there is the thread of epistemology, methodology and technique. Second, interwoven with it, is the theme of identifiable stages of research in terms like data gathering, analysis and writing up. I begin with the first.

In Chapter 3, I discussed the relationship between epistemology and methodology, saying that epistemology referred to what can be known and methodology to how to find it out. A methodology is made up of a number of methods and techniques: the methods are what are done in the research, and the methodology and epistemology give a rationale for doing so.[1] But the situation and its terminology are more confusing than this simple, logical story indicates, because of the range of views about how research should be carried out (see Part II for some of the reasons). Some rationales overlap with, and some overarch, other rationales. 'Qualitative' can be taken as describing methodology (see Chapter 1); so can 'feminist'. These two overlap: some qualitative research is feminist and some feminist research is qualitative. They also overarch or overlap other methodologies, such as life history, case study and action research. All of these can be qualitative and/or feminist, but need not be exclusively so.[2] A methodology indicates a set of methods, but these too overlap. Thus, all the methodologies mentioned could use participant observation, interviewing, recorded discussions and document analysis. Of course, some methods suit particular methodologies. But equally, there are methods which suit many methodologies.

The order of the questions in the logical framework should not be confused with when things happen in practice. Logically, the abstractions of epistemology come first, followed by methodology and finally methods and techniques. But this, chronologically and psychologically speaking, is hardly ever descriptive of research as it happens, where the order may be reversed, at least in the early stages, after which there are cycles of adjustment in understanding of methods, methodology and epistemology. During these cycles, the research is developed and refined. The initial design of Mehreen Mirza's research (described in Chapter 2) was determined for her. The method and some aspects of the methodology were given to her when she started. However, as her discussion shows, as the research proceeded, and as a result of working reflectively within these constraints, the methodology changed, as did the details of the methods she was using.

Similarly, Carrie Paechter (1993) provides an example of how to do research 'on the back of' contract research (intervention and evaluation). She was funded as part of a team to research the implementation of the new design and technology curriculum. The research changed its focus during the period of its funding, because of changes in national policy. This is quite a common occurrence in educational research, because events move so fast. Paechter was able, with the support of other team members, to use what looked like straightforward evaluation of the effects of policy, not only to deliver useful information to the funding agency, but also to develop a theory of power/knowledge in relation to interactions among teachers and their departments. Stronach *et al.* (1996) discuss undertaking contract research and effectively altering the methodological terms of the contract even while working within it. The two evaluation-research contracts they analyse could be described straightforwardly in traditional terms: the researchers used questionnaires with closed categories and computed response rates and types of responses. At the same time, they changed the methodology of the research by paying attention to transgressions and emotional expression in the ways the questionnaires were filled in by the respondents. These changes are described in non-traditional, postmodern terms, like 'transgressive validity' (Lather 1994). Clandinin and Connelly (1994) describe how the initial purposes of a piece of research can be altered by using the very methods those purposes dictated. All these examples show the principles in operation, as reflexivity (7 and 8), openness (3) and collaboration (4, 5 and 6) combine to move the research in the direction of research for social justice.

The second thread making up the logical framework is the set of stages of research. As with the order of epistemology, methodology and methods, these stages too have a logic, which should not be confused with what happens in practice.[3] The logic can be seen in the written sequence of most research reports, whether these are reports to sponsors, published articles or research theses. This reported order begins by identifying a question; moves through context (literature review and methodology); carries on with an account of how any empirical material was obtained and analysed; and ends up with conclusions, which may include some of the resultant dissemination and actions. A similar set of stages can be described for action research, but here they may be repeated in a series of cycles. Just as the methodology or methods are not decided once and for all, but continue to evolve, so it is with the stages of research. Nobody waits to conjecture about the practical outcomes of their research until after the analysis. Nobody completes the literature search before starting. Nor should they. All stages are revisable as understandings and values change – as of course they must. Research is meant to bring about precisely such change, generally and/or for the researcher personally.

Using the principles, the evolution of the stages of research can move the research in the direction of research for social justice. Reflexivity, openness, collaboration and consultation are all key features. I have given some examples from actual research reports of how research stages do not follow the apparently logical order. To show this, I focus on just one of the stages – the literature review – showing how decisions alter how it might really be carried out, whatever the apparent logic of the final report. The literature review is a key feature of any research report or thesis. It is meant to show significant work which influences the research and to point up the kinds of theoretical framework which drive the rest of the research. To show how the review is subject to the principles, not just at the start but all through the process of research, I discuss, briefly, how principle 6 (openness to view points of socio-political groups) and principle 7 (reflexivity about researchers' own socio-political position and interests) may apply.

As research continues, openness to view points of socio-political groups (principle 6) should lead to a greater awareness of a range of literature and theoretical framework springing from, say, feminist, anti-racist or post-colonial theory. This needs to be assessed, and whatever the researcher thinks of them, they need to be included in the literature. This can only come about as a result of doing the research. Thus, the final form of the literature review should be very different from the initial version, mirroring the growing sophistication of the researcher. This need not be presented in a deceptive manner. On the contrary, Mehreen Mirza and Melanie Walker's work, presented in Chapter 2, demonstrates how a growing understanding and awareness of different socio-political perspectives can permeate research.

Reflexivity about researchers' own interests (principle 7) is even harder, especially as it includes taking note of the career interests which are served by their production of the research. These are rarely served by paying attention to viewpoints of people from relatively marginalized groups – people from the very groups found through applying principle 6, explained in the previous paragraph. It is relatively easy to mention a few canonical names, but it is much harder to pay serious attention to less powerful and famous people. It is also likely that researchers' own socio-political positions within the academy mean that they are most likely to come into contact with the view points of relatively dominant groups. One way of dealing with this is to make strenuous efforts to seek out, use and acknowledge work by less fashionable, less mainstream authors. For some reports, Robin Richardson's 'Memorandum to oppressors' applies:

> Everyone peppers their discourse and conversation with bibliographical footnotes – references to people from whom they have learnt, and/or people who are big names. Make sure that you yourself, in your footnotes and references, give credit only to the oppressed. This means – amongst other things – that you should indeed reckon to have your mind nurtured only or mainly by the oppressed.
>
> (Richardson 1990: 206)

Collaboration for justice

I now turn to some details of the role of the researcher in relation to others: collaboration and its (dis)contents.[4] Attention is focused on the people immediately involved in the research, as researchers, subjects, advisors and gatekeepers (all of whom might be the same people). That is, in discussing collaboration, I focus on the issues raised by principle 4 (collaboration with those directly involved in the research) in particular, rather than those raised by principles 5 or 6 (openness to wider socio-political groupings and reflexivity about one's own). The related issues of insider–outsider research and ethical dilemmas are discussed in Chapter 9.

Why collaborate?

Behind principle 4, the principle of collaboration, as, indeed, behind all the principles, is the view that the role of an educational researcher is always to work in specific circumstances *with* rather than *on* or even *for* the people who inhabit them. This has, as I said in Chapter 4, some resonance with the concepts of being a 'specific intellectual' (Foucault 1980; Collins 1990); or an 'organic intellectual' (Gramsci 1971) in the context of feminism, anti-racism and social class analysis. Such a way of working is also a way of dealing with some of the arrogance presupposed in some forms of knowledge, and their implication in structures of dominance and oppression (see Chapter 5). Foucault (1980: 126) describes the role of the intellectual in his lecture 'Truth and power':

> For a long period, the 'left' intellectual spoke and was acknowledged the right of speaking in the capacity of master of truth and justice. He was heard, or purported to make himself heard, as the spokesman of the universal. To be an intellectual meant something like being the consciousness/conscience of us all . . .
> Some years have now passed since the intellectual was called upon to play this role . . . Intellectuals have got used to working . . . within specific sectors, at the precise points where their own conditions of life or work situate them (housing, the hospital, the asylum, the laboratory, the university, family and sexual relations) . . . This is what I would call the 'specific' intellectual as opposed to the 'universal' intellectual.

He goes on to explain the political and ethical implications. I quoted from him in Chapter 4 (page 60), arguing that even though truth and power cannot be separated, they can both be detached from dominant, hegemonic regimes of truth.

Foucault describes a kind of collaboration which could be called 'research with'. It is, however, only part of the story. What is missing from his otherwise compelling account is how research can also be 'research with', because it is *also* describable as 'research within'. Feminist and black researchers, for instance, are never within the master discourse. They may want, however, to speak to and against it. This kind of research could never have been neutral, universal or implicated in domination, in Foucault's sense. Rather, it is an attempt from outside the possibility of talking from a position of domination, to disrupt the master discourses. Michele Foster's description of her research study of the precise conditions of people working as black teachers in American schools shows this:

> The preponderance of negative portrayals of Black teachers written by outsiders, the contrasting more flattering and well-balanced insider descriptions, and the paucity of Black teachers telling their own stories convinced me of the need to augment the literature of Black teachers speaking in their own voices.

> (Foster 1994: 132)

She goes on:

> Research undertaken by scholars of color can be revisionist: it can offer new if disturbing insights, alternative and disquieting ways of thinking, can be a means of creating new paradigms and expanding existing ones, and can result in a much needed dialogue between scholars of color and their White peers. Regrettably, it is still the rule rather than the exception to distort and to exclude the realities and to subjugate the voices of people of color to further prevailing paradigms so as to fit the requirements of a caste society.

> (*ibid*.: 145)

What is collaboration?

If collaboration is to be a way of resolving these issues of developing research for justice, it has to be possible in practice. To see what this means, it is useful to look a little more closely at what kind of things are referred to as 'collaboration' in the context of doing research. There is a range of possibilities. There are methodologies in which collaboration is regarded as essential (or at least highly desirable) for proper research. Action research is one such. McTaggart (1994; McTaggart *et al.* 1997) gives a clear explanation of the significance of collaboration for action research, from the perspective of a university researcher working with teachers. Feminist research is another methodology in which collaboration is usually regarded as highly desirable, though as research within as much as research with. Riddell (1989) gives a brief, reflective overview of feminist perspectives on collaborative research.

To talk of collaboration in general is to say little about at what stage the collaboration takes place and how far it extends. There are a number of possibilities. For instance, it may take place only at the stage of identifying research topics, leaving the researcher to decide everything else about it. This is the kind of relationship envisaged, as I understand it, by those like David Hargreaves who want research to make an impact on the problems of teachers as a group. Against this, it could mean a commitment to support a group of teachers-as-researchers to carry out a school-based project in directions and with methods and evaluation criteria decided by them (Lomax

1991; Gitlin and Russell 1994; McTaggart *et al.* 1997). A further possibility is to be found in evaluative policy research, in which the policy-makers want to keep tight control over the form of the findings and their dissemination. Bell and Raffe (1991) give an entertaining and unusually open account of the kinds of problems raised by the relationship between researchers and policy-makers in the context of an evaluation of a government initiative.

Collaboration of a sort can take place at every research stage. At each stage, it may simply mean that the researcher has obtained permission from the subjects and stakeholders. Alternatively, it could mean the kind of joint enterprise where there is agreement between them over a particular stage of the investigation, be it research focus, data analysis or the final form of the report. It may also mean designing the research so that the research team is made up of people from a range of different backgrounds. They too can contribute at each or every stage of the research process, from conception through data collection to analysis and publication.

I am advocating collaboration in the context of getting social justice, as one of an interlocking set of principles. It is these other principles which provide the guidance about in what stages it takes place and with what degree of consensus, depending on circumstance. This is a matter for detailed judgement in the particular circumstances – circumstances which vary like the pattern in a kaleidoscope. This is true for all stages of research: here, I give just three extremely brief examples which are about dealing with drawing conclusions from data.

1 Sheila Riddell, rightly in my view, criticizes a collaboration that took into account only the views of the headmaster on a project, not those of any of the other staff.
2 At the same time, she gives reasons in terms of social justice for not attempting to get agreement to her findings about girls and physics from the boys and male teachers with whom she has been carrying out the research (Riddell 1989: 91).
3 Another way of dealing with different perspectives is by including different ones in the report. Thus Carol Davies and I speak in our voices as individuals, rather than as 'we', some of the time in our book about our project, *In Fairness to Children* (Griffiths and Davies 1995).

Bringing about collaboration: models of practice

Collaboration is fun, satisfying, motivating, mind-stretching and a way of working to one's strengths. At the same time, it is very difficult to do well. It may be a way of improving the justice of research, but if it is set up badly, it can go seriously wrong, ruining the chances of doing anything very useful. The difficulties are hardly ever discussed in published articles or books. There are very good personal, institutional and ethical reasons for this: it would be all too easy to offend (or even libel) colleagues. However, there is no doubt of the significance for the processes of research – this is why it is the stuff of so much anecdote and gossip, in sharp contrast to the silence of the published material. I, like everyone else, could tell my own stories, but don't – and won't – at least not in a form which would make their characters recognizable. However, I think it important at least to raise the issues, because of their significance for the actual possibilities of collaboration.

My stories are not all about me; and I am anonymizing, even in this very brief allusion to the reasons why collaboration can go wrong. A number of stories are about collaborations between individuals. The stories are about difficulties with colleagues: some have been determined to impose their own views, or used their power as research directors or as supervisors, or as influential in other arenas. Others are about imbalances of effort in joint enterprises: absent research directors, sloppy research assistance, non-existent contributions to reports that then have to be written by other members of the team. All this is exacerbated by the pressure to publish and get names on the front of reports or at the head of articles, regardless of effort – especially when some of the team are more powerful than others.

A number of stories are about collaborations between institutions. Partners have had unknown agendas which they have played close to their chests – and they, no doubt, have thought the same of us. However, all sides have had a stake in continuing to work together. Further, there have been difficulties between gatekeepers unwilling to allow any scrutiny of their institutions, even with the usual guarantees of anonymity and confidentiality; and with communications between directors and others, formally regarded as co-researchers, but also as less/more responsible, with less/more ownership and personal stake in the research. All this is criss-crossed with the effects of gender, race, social class, sexuality and disability on all these interactions.[5]

The catalogue of difficulties and dangers inherent in collaborative research can be understood in terms of the significance of power, and all the interlocking ways in which it works itself out. First, there are endless problems with power at levels of the personal, the institutional and the socio-political. Second, collaboration is often thought of on one of two models. Either the model is basically one of a level distribution of power, with everyone coming to an agreement (even if that works out as an agreement to tell the story in a number of equal but different voices), or the model is of a clear hierarchy of responsibility and control, but where those in control take some notice of or get some help from the other participants. Third, there are problems less with collaboration as joint action as with collaboration as guaranteeing enough cooperation for the research to proceed at all, even if not in a form envisaged by the participants (e.g. Walford 1991). In discussions of power at the beginning of this section (and in Chapter 4), I drew attention first to Foucault's analyses of how power relations were mobilized in particular local contexts, and second to feminist and anti-racist analyses focusing on sexism, racism and other large-scale formations of oppression. These analyses are useful in a discussion of collaboration in research for social justice.

The idea of collaboration – of joint theorizing and action – logically implies the existence of some kind of shared space in order that communication and joint action can happen. I propose a model in which this shared space is one which is public, but without necessarily being public to all. Schools provide a familiar example. School is often thought of as a public place, subject to public accountability, in contrast to the privacy of the home. On the other hand, it is also thought of as a place where children are protected from the public world, the world of work, into which they are to be inducted. However, this model is not most helpfully pictured in the popular image of a set of concentric circles, in which the outer is the most public (the world at large) and the central (a person's intimate circle) is the most private. Picture, instead, a set of intersecting cells, only some of which subsume others. In a school they might be: the school as a whole, a classroom, the staffroom, the playground, the football team, the drama club and the parents' room. It is important to notice that people in these cells are also members of invisible, imagined communities of identity, which are also cells: black, white, straight, gay, lesbian, old, young, middle-class, inner-city and so on. This kind of model is needed because, on the one hand, a collaboration brings together members of different cells in the sense of academics, teachers, managers, children, parents, social workers and so on, and also in the sense of men, women, Asians, Muslims and so on. The resulting collaboration forms a kind of cell itself. Its members are also members of their own cells, with powers of agency and the opportunity to mobilize powers within them. These groups may be able to act together in their cells or intersections of cells. So, again, there is a space to exert some power of agency and to mobilize power within it.

In this model, collaboration can be seen as a complex intersection of powers and mobilization of powers. It is not simply a collaboration of some more powerful group with some less powerful one (as some models of academic researchers and teachers imply). It also requires attention to be paid to the two kinds of cells that exist: those defined by face-to-face relations, usually of working life, and those defined by identifications of race, class, gender, sexuality and disability. The advantage of this model is that it allows for a clearer understanding of the reasons behind difficulties in collaboration, and the advantages of persevering. It gives a new way of understanding the issues behind distributing power 'evenly' or allocating responsibilities hierarchically. The question can then be asked: power to do what, where? This power could be found, for instance, in academic writing, in the classroom, in policy, in school management. Academics tend to focus on the significance of written publication, but it is action, not just publication, which is at issue – though publication is a kind of action. A good example of this kind of complexity is to be found in Somekh's analysis of the kinds of things that went on in her PALM project between teachers and academics as they negotiated all aspects of the research project (Somekh 1994). Another example of such an account is Kelly's reflective article about the Girls in Science and Technology Project (Kelly 1989).

Limits of collaboration

I have been discussing collaboration, showing how there are good reasons for setting it up. However, as I have made clear, these reasons are part of the principles as a whole, and may be overridden by other considerations. Thus, the principles show that the reasons for collaboration are: (a) to get action; (b) to get justice, through (i) getting others' perspectives, (ii) taking them seriously enough to be influenced by them and (iii) working together to implement action. However, there are cases where any of (i) (ii) or (iii) will be overridden by wider considerations of improvement and justice. I talk about some of the complexities of this again in later chapters. In the next chapter, I go into some of the details of taking other perspectives seriously in a discussion of empowerment and voice. In Chapter 9, the sections on ethics and insider–outsider research raise the issues of deception and hypocrisy.

Notes

1 I use the terms 'method' and 'technique' interchangeably, and distinguish both from 'methodology'. See Harding (1988) for an admirably clear, succinct explanation of this.
2 Except in the generous definition of qualitative research I gave in Chapter 1, which included any research that made some use of non-numerical data. But here I refer to the narrower definitions of qualitative research that, as I said in Chapter 1, generate so much heat and dust.
3 Note that Clandinin and Connelly's methodological remarks about research methods influencing the purposes of the research as well as vice versa, was made in a chapter in the section of Denzin and Lincoln's (1994) collection entitled '*Methods of collecting and analyzing empirical materials*' (my italics). In practice, their methods determined their methodology as well as the other way round. Yet, interestingly in this article they preserve much of the usual written logic of research articles. They begin with methodological remarks before proceeding to discuss methods.
4 I am referring to Freud's famous book title, *Civilisation and Its Discontents*. He argued, roughly, that civilization was to be approved and worked for – but that it could drive you mad.
5 For something about all this at international level, see Griffiths and Parker-Jenkins (1994).

8 | Getting justice: empowerment and voice

Justice, power and empowerment

The terms 'power' and 'empowerment' crop up a great deal in research related to social justice. This is not surprising. Improvements in justice are related to power: who has it, how it is exercised and where it manifests itself. It sounds as if researchers for social justice would find a lot to agree about here. But this is not the case. The use of the terms can obscure profound disagreements about what to do, rooted in disagreements of theory. At the same time, the terms can be useful in that they draw attention to a fundamental agreement about the importance of altering power relations in order to enhance justice. Further, the very differences invite greater reflexivity and clarity about what researchers think they are doing, and whether it is worthwhile. This is of practical importance all through the research; from the start (clarifying the aims, designing the methods) to the end (evaluating its worth, and deciding on future actions). It is worth noting, for instance, the significance of 'power' and power relations in all the examples of research for social justice described in Chapter 2 – including in my critiques of them. David Gillborn and Caroline Gipps's overview of research is, precisely, framed by the category of ethnicity and race: these are categories which are significant precisely because of the power relations they signal. Mehreen Mirza's methodology is based, methodologically, in a theoretical understanding of power. Stephen Ball's analytical framework depends on power as a central category. Melanie Walker evaluates her own research in terms like 'oppression' and 'emancipation'.

The concept of 'empowerment' is popular in educational research. Some examples demonstrate the range of claims to be undertaking research for empowerment. They show that it is not the prerogative of any one view of the politics of research. First, central to liberalism is a belief in the usefulness of knowledge to gain power and to use it wisely, as I discussed in relation to Bacon's and Comte's view that 'knowledge is power' (Chapter 4). But

Weiner (1994: 68, 79) traces the significance of 'empowerment' and a concern with power relations within radical *as opposed to* liberal feminist research. Lather, from her postmodern perspective (neither liberal nor radical; which sprang from, but is critical of, Marxism), explores the possibilities of research, given her stated assumption that: 'an emancipatory social science must be premised upon the development of research approaches which both empower the researched and contribute to the generation of change enhancing social theory' (Lather 1988: 293). David Gillborn, from a position critical of the politics of postmodernism, concludes that: 'it is essential that we keep asking difficult questions – *about who has power; who wins; who loses?*' (Gillborn 1997: 357). The range is even wider than this. Usher and Edwards (1994) point out the significance of empowerment as an aim of both humanistic psychology and critical pedagogy, while Siraj-Blatchford (1994) argues that empowerment is put forward as an aim for researchers variously influenced by feminism, action research and radical pedagogy.

Most of these different views do not engage much with each other. However, there have been some attempts to help the research community to gain in reflexivity and clarity about the possibilities of empowerment, and the different assumptions and arguments about power which underlie them. Jennifer Gore's book on critical and feminist pedagogies has been very influential. Her research project was situated in her own practice as a teacher educator, committed to both critical pedagogy and feminist pedagogy. In investigating the contradictions of her own practice, and the assumptions that underlie them, she uses Foucault's notion of 'regimes of truth', and the power relations they embody as they tend towards universalization and domination (Gore 1993: xv). Gore's criticisms have proved helpful in clarifying notions of power and empowerment which underlie research strategies as well as pedagogies. She points out that underlying both feminist and critical pedagogy is 'a notion of power as property', which can be used or given away by an agent that has it, in order to achieve 'a vision or desired end state' (*ibid.*: 121). (She claims that this is implicit in the word 'em-powerment' itself.) She argues that this gives a dual conception of power, as 'repressive but reclaimable for productive and democratic purposes'. Gore argues that this conception is flawed, because it is built around a misleading analysis of power, which ignores institutional and discursive constraints. She further argues that feminist and critical pedagogies have failed to deliver empowerment of the kind they want, because of these flaws. She also criticizes the claims of action research to be transformative and emancipatory on the grounds that it usually has very little influence over the whole context; nor do all its practitioners even take on its emancipatory aims. She is working on the development of an alternative using a Foucauldian analysis which takes relational notions of power into account within the institutional context of pedagogy (Gore 1993, 1997).

The criticism has been very useful in generating more reflexivity and clarity. For instance, Robin McTaggart and his colleagues, writing from within the paradigm of participatory action research, defend its claims against Gore's criticisms. They reflect on a project in which they were all involved. The purpose of the project was to transform a school's bureaucratic review process into participatory action research for the improvement of educational practice within the school (McTaggart *et al.* 1997). They draw on Seyla Benhabib's (1992) analysis to argue for 'weak theses' of postmodernism which leave room for agency and for the possibility of improvement and progress. In evaluating a project designed around the process of School Review, they say:

> Whether things are better is not always an easy question to answer, but it is the primary question participants in an action research programme need to answer for themselves when they are deciding whether to continue. Of course, these teachers don't lay claim to 'emancipation' largely because they would probably regard such talk as self-regarding. . . . While importing action research as part of a bureaucratic process of review, created confusion, it was valued as a form of resistance and redirection. The teachers don't discuss the hegemony of bureaucratic intervention in those terms, but they seem to know what to do about it.
>
> (McTaggart *et al.* 1997: 136–7)

Barry Troyna (1995) takes up some of Gore's criticisms in relation to other forms of research for social justice. Drawing on her analysis, he argues that educational researchers make the mistake of basing their work on all three of the following assumptions: (a) that the notion of empowerment does not need explanation or definition; (b) that researchers know what disempowers the subjects of their research; and (c) that the researchers are then able to empower those subjects, with the result that they are no longer disempowered. He is critical of claims by a number of researchers that their research contributes to the empowerment of their subjects. Like McTaggart *et al.*, they seem well able to defend themselves against these charges.[1] However, the article is extremely useful, in that it opens up a space for such issues to be debated, and the different assumptions of researchers to be measured against each other.

The concept of 'empowerment' is ambiguous between different conceptions of power. There are a range of meanings of 'power', some of them incompatible with others. Some of this range can be seen in even the first paragraph of this chapter, where I hedged some of my bets by talking not only of 'who has it' and 'who exercises it', but also of 'how it manifests itself'. In Chapter 4, I pointed out that power could be understood as personal power over somebody else, and discussed in relation to 'authority' – this is the liberal view. Or, in a more socialist or Marxian view, power is exercised through cultural and economic means, which act on the thoughts and desires of whole social classes. Alternative to both of these is the Foucauldian analysis of power manifesting itself in the micro circulations of dominance and resist-ance, being constituted in the actions, procedures and bodies of specific social contexts.

These different meanings and views of power underlie different views about what would count as empowerment from different paradigms of research. So, not surprisingly, 'empowerment' means something different depending on the underlying conceptions of power. These differences are useful if they lead to constructive exchanges of views and perceptions: to reflexivity and more clarity. But it is very difficult for those researchers who get caught in the noise and smoke of paradigm wars but who only want to know what to do as researchers in the face of injustice. They are helped by being aware of different possibilities.

A schematic examination of the possibilities of the meanings attached to 'empowerment' is a first step. As I pointed out, the possibilities include the traditional notions derived from Bacon's and Comte's 'knowledge is power'. However, these days, the notion of empowerment is more likely to be invoked by those who do not regard themselves as positivist, liberal or empiricist.[2] This still leaves a great range. Claims to research leading to people 'being empowered' or even just 'feeling empowered' include those based on the individual (or small group of individuals) coming to act expres-sively and on principle. This seems to be a notion based on personal agency, though sometimes within a Foucauldian analysis of positionality.

Some examples of a highly personal interpretation of empowerment are to be found in action research. In Chapter 2, I summarized Melanie Walker's action research report, 'Doing action research in South Africa', in which she reflects on the possibility that her action research into the facilitation of teacher development could lead to emancipatory actions. In the course of this report, she discusses teacher development in terms of the personal pos-itioning of individual teachers. She gives an example of one teacher's per-sonal development from 'a teacher working in isolation behind the private walls of her classroom' to 'developing competence in co-operative relations with others' (Walker 1995: 21) as somebody with something to teach others, as well as somebody with something to learn from them. From the United States, Andrew Gitlin (a university professor) and Robyn Russell (a class-room teacher) evaluate a collaborative project in which a central aim was to develop research which was evaluated in terms of 'the degree to which it enables disenfranchised groups to fully participate in the decision-making process' (Gitlin and Russell 1994: 187). This evaluation considered how far Robyn Russell had, individually, changed the terms of the decision-making process, as well as considering the rest of the teachers in the school. In Britain, a special issue of the *British Educational Research Journal* focused on methodological and empowerment issues in practical teacher research (O'Hanlon 1995). The widespread use in this collection of autobiographical personal accounts demonstrates how many of the projects make a personal interpretation of empowerment.

Second, there are socialist-Marxian interpretations underpinning the claim that empowerment comes about with the loss of a false consciousness combined with the resultant opportunities for organization among people with common political interests who exercise their agency. This claim can be found in research drawing on critical pedagogy (McLaren 1994; Weiler 1994) and on Gramsci (Siraj-Blatchford 1994). For instance, Vincent (1996) draws on both Gramsci and Freire in her study of parents and their possible participation in schools. She criticizes those models of parental participation which lead to individual solutions, on the grounds that they allow no space for the development of a collective voice. In an article written with Tomlinson, concern is expressed about the small chances of parents 'developing a collective voice and engaging in broader political challenges of perceived injustices' (Riddell and Vincent 1997: 254). In this, they are concerned with parents organizing in relation to the structures of class and gender, not just as individuals (Vincent and Tomlinson 1997).

Third, there are interpretations which link empowerment to 'voice'. This may be a collective interpretation or a more personal one. Vincent (1996) uses the concept of 'voice' in both an individual and collective sense. She talks of the 'collective parental voice' but also acknowledges that a parent can influence events through a highly individualized one. The concept of voice has been influential in feminist and black theories. These theories bring together the personal and collective, since the individual black or woman's voice is now to be understood within the collectivity of black or woman's voices. However, as I shall point out in the next section, 'voice' covers as many kinds of meanings as 'empowerment'.

Lastly, poststructuralist research, usually drawing on Foucault, emphasizes the context and relationship aspects of power, so that empowerment is about the place of the agent within the context of their discourse and institution. In her investigations of girls and education, Walkerdine uses poststructuralist analysis to investigate the positionality of girls, and of working-class girls in particular, in relation to their perceived success at mathematics (Walkerdine 1990). Similarly, Sewell (1996a, b) develops a poststructuralist analysis of the performance of black boys in schools. He draws on the perceptions of teachers and of the boys themselves about their current relationships to power, in order to investigate the possibility of their moving into new ones.

A schematic account can be useful, but it must be recognized that it is schematic. The distinctions that I have drawn are based on the rather more complex account in Chapter 4, and that, too, is oversimplified.[3] In particular, the distinctions should not be read as signifying discrete categories: that there is a choice of either/or between them. On the contrary, the categories are just as likely to be 'both/and' as 'either/or'. For instance, I, myself, assert the importance of agency, but in recognition of its limitations. Thus, for me, in the context of action research, empowerment has to be understood within the circulations of power in a local context; as do the possibilities of that changed agency in repositioning and reconfiguring those circulations. Melanie Walker (1996a: 422–3) takes much the same view:

> Small-scale self-aware action, one step at a time, does constitute accountable educational action for social change . . . Practitioners in the field . . . might use their hybrid positioning to work for them in constructing alternative discourses which problematise dominant lines of power.

Donald *et al.* in what is, significantly, a *special issue* of the *British Educational Research Journal* on 'methodological and empowerment issues', take much the same view:

> Action research of this kind is about generating personal and local knowledge that can be translated into the leverage of power. Or, to put it in a more sophisticated kind of way, it is about the power already inherent in those kinds of new knowledge, in that kind of redefinition of the problem, in that changed recognition of ourselves as professionals.
>
> (Donald *et al.* 1995: 272)

On the other hand, some of the other contributors to *Special Issue* (O'Hanlon 1995) take a much more individualized view of what constitutes 'empowerment' (Lally and Scaife 1995; Pryor 1995). Stephen Ball asserts a somewhat similar 'both/and' in the context of his policy research:

> Ethnography is a way of engaging critically with, and developing interpretations of, 'the real'. Like [Foucauldian] genealogy it is disruptive, it is often about giving voice to the unheard, it also about the play of power-knowledge relations in local and specific settings . . .
>   I recognize that I am straddling somewhat uncomfortably, a crucial epistemological divide . . . I am also not unwilling to admit my ambivalence about certain versions of post-structuralism, to own up to a modernist commitment to the idea of 'the real' and to the constraints of the material context, or to wanting to retain some version of purposive agency.
>
> (Ball 1994: 4)

With the caution about oversimplifications in mind, some further useful schematic distinctions can be drawn. The parameters within which empowerment is discussed can be arranged in three phases. *First*, it can be seen that the possibility of empowerment is something that is ascribed to individuals, groups, classes of people, or discursive social contexts. *Second*, the power that accrues in each case can be found in the ability to act on and/or to change a situation directly, or it can be a more personal, experiential affair to be found in the consciousness and understanding. Of course, for the latter to be possible, there has to be a theoretical possibility of agency. *Third*, the underlying metaphor of power can be in terms of matter or form. It can be assumed to be a kind of stuff which can be handed from one person or group to another. (This is Gore's concept of 'power as property'.) Such a view results in an exchange of power being a kind of zero-sum transaction, though there are differences within that about whether the property has been given away, leased, given on condition or grabbed. The Foucauldian conception of micro circulations of power, a kind of productivity of power, generates no such zero-sum game. Here, as forces act on and through individuals, it is more appropriate to talk of leverage, as Donald *et al.* do in the quotation above. Alternative metaphors might be 'surfing the circulations', or 'dancing with the discourses'. Power as collaborative is another form of the productivity of power which does not have to be understood in terms of zero-sum games. While power which is the result of collaboration might reduce power somewhere else (as, for instance, in social action) it can also generate quite new actions and contexts which have their being outside previous forms of power.

The reason for looking at all these different conceptions of power and empowerment has been to give some guidance to educational researchers for social justice. In the previous two chapters I put forward ten principles for social justice precisely in order to offer such guidance. The ten principles are not neutral between different conceptions of power, because a view of power underpins them (see Part II). However, I believe they are compatible with some other views, and so still useful even for a researcher who holds a different view of power, though with some reservations. Thus, anyone holding to a view dependent on universal emancipation and certainty would have to use them with caution. From my perspective, methods and actions built around those views fit, but only if they are seen as special cases that work locally rather than universally. An analogy here would be with Newton's laws of gravity being a special case of Einstein's general theory of relativity. Newton's laws work very well for earth-size objects. Another analogy would be with a flat earth being a good theory for local application (for instance, in designing a garden) but not so good as distances increase. The point here is to be clear about what is being claimed for empowerment by research. The parameters I have given are helpful in clarifying the scope of the theory and the assumptions about power that underlie it. The claims can then be evaluated against the principles of research for social justice.

The principles are interlocking, as explained before. Uncertain knowledge and fallible, risky justice underpin them all, as is clear in principles 1 and 2. However, that uncertainty is mitigated by a cheerful acceptance of continuing effort. This is especially evident from principle 9: there is no hope of perfection and utopia does not exist. This effort is guided by the necessity of paying attention to other perspectives (principles 4, 5 and 6). It will not be surprising if those perspectives result in the raising of such questions as: power for what, by whom, when, in whose interest, with what long-term consequences? Chapter 7 drew attention to the significance of asking such questions in the context of setting up collaborative research. They are equally important at other stages of research, including data collection, data analysis and writing up the results. Which of these is most significant depends on the relative emphasis given to, say, personal change, voice or action.

Voice and empowerment

Closely related to debates about power and empowerment are debates about power and 'voice'. Indeed, 'voice' is probably as popular as 'empowerment' in research related to social justice. Gitlin and Russell (1994) emphasize its importance to those teachers working in schools who feel that they have relatively little influence over the course of research. They advocate a dia-logical relationship between university and school-based researchers such as themselves (Gitlin is professor of educational studies at the University of Utah; Russell is an elementary school teacher in Salt Lake City, Utah). They explain why:

> A dialogical process where participants negotiate meanings at the level of question posing, data collection, and analysis . . . The central moti-vation for encouraging a dialogical process is that it can further the aim of developing voice among those who have been silenced historically . . . But the notion of voice can go far beyond the opportunity to speak: it can be about protest. Understood in this way, voice becomes politi-cized.
>
> (Gitlin and Russell 1994: 185–6)

This aim is only partly realized in their work, as they acknowledge. While the individual teacher and some of her colleagues develop a voice, the impact of the school-based project remains limited:

> Nothing about the physical work conditions of the teachers changed . . . All the common constraints that . . . limit most types of consistent examination of educational issues were still in place . . . All the changes taking place are at school level.
>
> (*ibid.*: 198, 200)

It is obvious, though, that despite these stringent self-criticisms, they both still value the voice that has been developed.

The link with 'empowerment' is clear. Like 'empowerment', 'voice' can refer to something individual and personal, or it can mean something far more collective, social and overtly political. The quotation from Stephen Ball (1994) in the previous section shows that it can also mean something less attached to human beings, more contextual and discursive. As with 'empowerment', when these differences are not made explicit and recognized, the situation can be very confusing to researchers wanting to know what to do for the best. It is not surprising, then, that a section of Troyna's (1995) article about empowerment discusses the question of 'voice'.

Troyna is critical of the idea that voice is supposed to be empowering. He uses Bhavani (1988) to draw a distinction between 'empowerment' and 'giving a voice'. She points out how 'giving a voice' by using, for instance, direct speech extracts in a piece of ethnographic research is disempowering rather than empowering. She points out cases in which 'giving a voice' masks the power inequalities in the research, while conferring a dimension of authenticity to the damaging stereotypes it reproduces.[4] In her response, Iram Siraj-Blatchford argues that Troyna is confusing arguments against merely quoting the direct speech of research respondents with research strategies in which respondents are 'given the opportunity to "talk back" ' (Siraj-Blatchford 1994: 25). Her use of bell hooks' phraseology ('talk back') signals the feminist–anti-racist nature of her argument. She goes on, drawing on the critical pedagogy of Freire and on Gramsci:

> Black readers who remember the time when they were 'given their colour' will have no problems with this concept . . . What is important is finding a 'voice' that engages in critical reflection, in resistance to domination, and in affirmation of the liberation struggle.
>
> (*ibid.*: 25)

It is this kind of view that motivates Michele Foster's research, described in Chapter 7. Her concluding section drives this home:

> By using the personal histories . . . of members of the Black community and framing them in theoretical and conceptual perspectives that gave voice to their realities, it was my hope to contribute to . . . empowerment of Black communities . . .
>
> There were many times when I interacted with my subjects that I heard my own voice in theirs, voices that had waged a continuing struggle against an analysis of their lives imposed by outsiders . . . seeking to reorder their realities to conform to an external agenda.
>
> (Foster 1994: 145)

This discussion is asymmetrical. Troyna's argument, like Bhavani's, is focused most sharply on the uses to which white researchers might put the words of black research subjects. On the other hand, Siraj-Blatchford and Foster argue about voice, as black researchers drawing on their own experiences of research. It is clear that much of this argument turns on the position of the researcher as 'insider' or 'outsider' to the community being researched – and whether or not that community has a voice already. I say more about the issues surrounding insider-outsiders in the next chapter.

However, this is not the whole story. The argument is also about the kind of connection there might be between individuals and their 'voices' on the one hand, and empowerment on the other. Using the term 'voice' signifies more than the expression of an isolated individual's opinion, what might be called 'speech'. As Siraj-Blatchford and Foster make clear, the development of voice is contingent upon identification with others, in a group marked by its relation to power: marked by sexuality, race, religion, gender, social class.[5] This is, of course, not an exercise in choral speaking. Rather, voice is made up of the weaving together of individual expressions, in the understanding that individuals are constructed by, as well as constructing, the social contexts in which they live (see Chapter 5, pages 80–3).

It is the identification with others that has a long-term effect on voice; and on discourse, social action, possibilities of actions and influence on others – in short, on politics. The kind of self-understanding that comes from identification with others in a group is not independent of, or even necessarily prior to, the collective actions of what is traditionally understood as 'social action'. 'The personal is the political' was a slogan for the early feminist movement, and the insight that it encapsulated has been central to other liberation movements, including both black scholarship (Fanon 1952; Gilroy 1993) and the politics of sexuality (Epstein 1994; Biddulph 1996). Some of the reasons for the political significance of self-interpretations brought about by joining or creating a group were noted in Chapter 4 (pages 52–4). In relation to voice, it is worth noting the significance of cultural politics (such as being given colour) and academic reflection (using the lens of sexuality, social class or disability, for instance), as well as of collective action, in bringing about lasting changes in relation to educational practice.[6]

It is now possible to see that there are a number of different understandings of 'voice' that need to be distinguished. Like the concepts of 'empowerment', they are characterized by being 'both/and' as often as 'either/or' in relation to each other. One kind of 'voice' can contribute to another, but they should not be mistaken for each other. 'Voice' is also like 'empowerment' in the dimensions which describe these different conceptions. *First* is who (or what) it is ascribed to: individuals, political groupings or, as Stephen Ball suggests, 'the unheard' in terms of ideas, perspectives and metaphors available in discourse. *Second*, there is the relation of voice to power, in terms of agency, change and discursive formations. *Third* are the underlying metaphors of form or substance: just as power can be thought of as a kind of stuff in a zero-sum transaction, voice can be thought of in terms of airtime or volume in a competitive struggle to get a hearing; or it may be conceptualized as creative and productive, developing a greater richness of sound, with new themes and harmonies interwoven in the old.

This analysis serves to give some handle on the difference between research which is exploitative of the offered speech and voices of the researched and that which is not. For instance, Mac an Ghaill's (1988) study of racism was one of the pieces of research criticized by Troyna as being about voice, but not empowerment. Mac an Ghaill undertook participant observation of the positionality of Asian and Afro-Caribbean students in a school and a college. As this study progressed, he developed a complex, dynamic relationship with the students, which developed into a collaborative model. Mac an Ghaill (1991: 113) explains this in his reflective article on his methodology: 'As my research developed, I moved to a collaborative model that involved the students, their parents and other members of the black community, in generating empirical data, and formulating and validating theory.' This project and the reflection on it is one of the studies criticized by Troyna (1995) as being about voice rather than about empowerment. This criticism fails to recognize that the student's point of view was represented not only in a way that they agreed with, but also within a politicized framework which indicates that the research had, if anything, helped in their development of voice. Even more striking is that Mac an Ghaill presents evidence that the views of the students, and his interaction with them, changed his own theoretical framework – the very framework which was used to analyse and present the data. It is significant that Mac an Ghaill is concerned to be clear about the complexities of voice and empowerment, including the possibilities and pitfalls:

> I was acutely conscious of this dilemma [of black people being the subjects of white research] . . . A problem that remained throughout the research was the feeling of 'ripping off' the students. Asking the students about this, two of the Rasta Heads, Kevin and Leslie, sarcastically suggested that I had probably 'saved them' from other white liberals . . . who 'visited Kilby to help them!'
>
> (Mac an Ghaill 1991: 115–16)

There are practical consequences for researchers in their understanding of 'empowerment' and 'voice'. Gitlin and Russell, for instance, like Foster, were clear enough about what kind of empowerment and voice they wanted to generate for their reflective articles to allow them – and us – to evaluate their successes. These examples show how all the processes of research can be affected by the particular conceptions of 'voice' and 'empowerment' which underpin them, including the initial design and then the data collection, analysis and dissemination. Mac an Ghaill (1991: 106 115) gives some examples:

> I had not intended to carry out a study of black female students. In fact it would be more accurate to say that they chose me. I met a small group of black female students, of Asian and Afro-Caribbean parentage, at a sixth form college where I was teaching sociology. I discussed the study

of the Rasta Heads . . . They were enthusiastic about the findings but were critical of the absence of the discussion of gender relations . . .

The more positive involvement of the Kilby School students in my work was decisively aided by Parminder and Gilroy, two key participants, who were respected and trusted by the other students. They became unofficial research assistants.

These last two quotations nicely illustrate how the principles for educational research for social justice work together. In looking at empowerment and voice, I have been focusing most closely on the first principle: 'A main reason for doing the research is to get improvement in social justice in and from education.' One such improvement is related to power and voice. Since the principles are interlocking, this can be seen in the other principles too, which focus on who has a say, whose viewpoints count and the socio-political dimensions of all this, and whether the researcher, and everyone else, is prepared to change their minds as a result of coming into contact with alternative perspectives.

Notes

1 I say 'they' but I should say 'we', because I am included, along with Mac an Ghaill and a number of others.
2 Though see warnings in Troyna (1995) about the politics of the Right and the danger of their appropriating the rhetoric of empowerment.
3 See Chapter 4, note 7.
4 See also Opie (1992). Michelle Fine (1994) develops the useful concept of 'ventriloquism', in which a researcher chooses extracts from the data which make her respondents appear to speak for themselves, but which are actually chosen to underpin her own perspectives. No one is suggesting that this can be avoided completely, of course. The point is how far the perspectives of the researcher are open to change and dissension in the voices she has collected.
5 I might have included 'being a teacher', as Gitlin and Russell argue, or a child at school, as we argue in Griffiths and Davies (1995).
6 I discuss this in much more detail in 'Changing selves', Chapter 10 of my *Feminisms and the Self: the Web of Identity* (Griffiths 1995a).

9 | Better knowledge

Introduction

The subject of this chapter is 'better knowledge'. Educational research – all research – is about getting knowledge. As the first two principles of educational research for social justice state, the two main reasons for doing the research are: to get improvements in social justice, in and from education; and to get knowledge and to learn from it. This is 'better knowledge' in two senses of 'better': knowledge which can be relied on and knowledge which can be used wisely, to a good purpose. These two principles are underpinned by a view of social justice and a view of knowledge and power which are expressed in the other eight principles. They emphasize the uncertainty of knowledge, and the importance of collaboration, of openness to other perspectives and of reflexivity.

In Part II, and especially in Chapter 5, I outlined an approach to epistemology, but it was in very abstract terms. Here I connect that discussion with the more concrete questions facing researchers, in terms in which they are likely to be challenged. The mainstream is likely to pose challenges in terms of bias and validity. Minority groups, whether as subjects or researchers, are more likely to be concerned with these questions of bias and validity in different terms, talking instead of the contradictions of being a researcher from a marginal group, exploitation by outsiders, co-option into the academy and the responsibilities of insiders. I address these issues in the sections on ethical issues and insider–outsider research.

Bias, validity and reliability

All researchers have opinions about what they are researching. Their research has been chosen precisely because it is something of significance to them (unless they simply needed the job). Opinions give a clue to values.

They are views about what the research will show and why it matters. Part of the point of the research is to test them out against what Miles and Huberman (1984: 38) have called 'the lovely imperfection and intractability of the field'. In the context of the principles of research for social justice, we should add 'and the lovely intractability of the existence of other people who see things their way'. Opinions set the research off and motivate it.

Do opinions bias research? Bias is something to be avoided in any paradigm of research. All researchers try to avoid it, because all researchers hold to common values that are internal to *any* research process. These are values related to impartiality, elegance of solutions, coherence with previous results, criticality, openness and painstaking use of procedures. Not surprisingly, there is disagreement among researchers about what *counts* as impartiality, elegance and the rest. These values are sometimes discussed in technical terms, such as validity and reliability, but, again, there is considerable disagreement among researchers about what counts as validity or reliability. In Chapter 4, I commented that researchers were sometimes expected to keep their opinions to themselves, so as not to bias the research. I argued there that this view was mistaken, because without some acknowledgement of initial opinions, including beliefs and values, the research will certainly be biased. The point here is to note that opinions start, but do not end, the research. In other words, your research should be able to surprise you. Otherwise, it certainly is biased.

Bias in research can appear at three levels. There is: (a) bias within any specific research process in terms of the rigorous use of procedures and criticality; (b) bias related to the values and politics of the researchers which inform which of these procedures are followed; (c) bias in the wider context of research. (These three levels correspond, roughly, to the categories of technique, methodology and epistemology – the last in relation to power/knowledge, as discussed in Chapter 7 and in Part II.) Within these three levels, there are particular issues that are relevant to social justice, and it is only these that I focus on in this book. Discussions of the other issues can be found in many general books on research methods. It is unfortunate that few of these books address social justice issues directly, or even at all.[1]

Bias within a specific research process

There is a huge range of techniques and processes used in educational qualitative research at all stages of the research process. There are different forms of collecting data, and of analysing them; and there is a range of techniques used in writing up the analysis and reporting on the research. All of these are subject to general principles of research with respect to avoiding bias and working towards validity and reliability in the use of evidence (even though the precise meanings of the terms 'bias', 'validity' and 'reliability' are themselves always in question). These can be made concrete with respect to particular techniques, such as, to mention just four to show the range, using documents, structured observations, doing an analysis with the help of software designed to handle large quantities of data or writing an ethnography.[2]

Using general principles is not enough, however, especially given the range of interpretations of bias, validity and reliability in qualitative research. Any techniques used need to be applied and interrogated using the principles for social justice. Principles 6 and 7 are particularly relevant: openness to perspectives of socio-political groups, and reflexivity about the positionality of the researchers. To illustrate this, I will have a brief look at a technique of data collection (interviewing) and at two kinds of validity used at the stage of analysis.

Interviewing is a common technique of data gathering, and is used in a number of different methodologies. Sources of bias are discussed in standard texts, which talk of factors such as: sample frames (and the labelling of narrow samples as narrow); access; the significance of non-verbal communication, trust and rapport; and the effect of any previous or continuing relationship between interviewer and interviewed (such as teacher and taught). From the perspective of social justice, this list needs extending and deepening. What are missing are factors explicitly related to the positionality of the researchers and their openness to other perspectives. In fact, these two affect all of these factors.

The positionality of all the participants, research subjects and any advisors, as well as of the research team, are significant in the process of the research. This can hardly be surprising to anybody. Race and gender (and social class, disability and sexuality, when they are visible) are so salient in any human interactions in this society that they are obviously likely to affect communication during an interview. However, only a few of the standard research methods texts make some mention of the race and gender of the participants, and even fewer of social class, sexuality or disability. Even when they do, the tendency is to assume that these are additional factors, rather than being constitutive of all the factors. A further temptation is to assume that such factors are relevant only in research directly about social justice. This is a mistake. After all, access and the way interviewer and interviewee construct each other will vary depending on the self-identifications of the interviewer, and this is just as true for interviews about, say, school leadership as it is for interviews about girls and technology.

The principle of being open to the perspectives of different socio-political groups will help researchers to avoid both temptations. Such groups often term themselves 'marginal' or 'excluded', indicating how they feel shut out from the dominant processes of communication. Openness to the perspectives of such groups would quickly indicate how an unreflective approach to the factors of sampling frames or to access procedures either excludes them or over-represents them. In particular, they often find that they are the stereotypical subjects of a piece of research, or are missing altogether. It is striking how often management, policy or curriculum research ignores the factors of gender, race and sexuality, though each factor can readily be found in research on classroom interaction, exclusions and health education, respectively. (In Chapter 2, I pointed out the significance of social justice even when the research is 'about' something else.) Groups can be narrow on the grounds of gender, race, sexuality (etc.), whether the interviews are 'about', say, school management, science education or the implementation of equal opportunities. Other factors are similarly affected.

Deciding what to do about the effects of these factors is not straight-forward and the decision has to be judged within the principles as a whole. For instance, I was part of a team carrying out research into teachers' and pupils' views of the schooling of Pakistani-Muslim pupils. Access was severely constrained by the gatekeepers. Groups of children and teachers were chosen for us, for instance. But while we had only limited control, we were able to note this in the report and allow for it in the conclusions. In relation to the identity of the interviewers, we had more control. We judged that the white teachers were best interviewed by white teachers, while the pupils were interviewed by young British-born Asian interviewers, who helped to construct the questions. This was a decision related to the judg-ments we made on how the attitudes and beliefs of the interviewers would be perceived by our respondents.

'Face validity' and 'respondent validity' are related terms which are often invoked in the analysis of qualitative data. The meanings commonly attached to these terms need to be interrogated using the principles of social justice, because these meanings are so open to interpretation. 'Face validity' is one way of assessing whether the findings are 'really about what they appear to be about' in terms of 'what seems reasonable' (Robson 1993: 66, 68). Hitchcock and Hughes (1995: 105) call this a way of judging: 'descrip-tive validity . . . the extent to which the research describes what, in fact, the study set out to do and describe and whether this description was accurate and authentic'. They go on to say: 'Very often people will judge such work [ethnographic research] in terms of the apparently soft notion of face valid-ity. Do the descriptions ring true? Do they feel right?' (*ibid.*: 106). This term obviously overlaps with 'respondent validity', which is validation by taking data and analysis back to the subject to check their accuracy. Similar sug-gestions for judging validity come from Hammersley (1995), in terms of the research being 'plausible' and 'credible'.

The question raised from the perspective of social justice is: whose judge-ment counts here? To whom, exactly, should it seem reasonable, right and plausible? The dominant view is often exactly what research for social jus-tice is challenging, so it would be very surprising if the research was imme-diately seen as 'reasonable', 'right' or 'plausible' to stakeholders in the dominant view. In Chapter 7, I mentioned Riddell's criticism of a piece of research in a school, in which the view of the headteacher was canvassed, but not the views of the rest of the staff or the pupils. This was validation by relatively more powerful members of the school. In contrast, the results of Sewell's research into the performance of black boys in school was taken back to both boys and staff in a number of schools (including the case study school). The reactions of the boys in particular have been taken seriously in further reports and analysis of the research results (Sewell 1996a, b). The principles of social justice give some guidance on which groups should have their opinions sought about what seems 'right', 'reasonable', 'plausible' or 'credible'. Ideally, they include (a) all concerned with the research, even if not directly the community carrying out the research, and (b) various socio-political groups.[3]

Bias related to the values and politics of the researcher

This kind of bias refers to my argument in Chapter 5 that bias comes not from having ethical and political positions – this is inevitable – but from not acknowledging them. Not only does such acknowledgement help to unmask any bias that is implicit in those views, but it also helps to provide a way of responding critically and sensitively to the research. This is a different point from that of the previous section, which focused on the *position* of the researchers and other participants. This argument is about their espoused values and beliefs. Thus, researchers need to recognize not only the partiality of all perspectives (which was the argument in the previous section), but also their own espoused values and politics.

The need to take individuals' values and politics seriously has implications for a single researcher. More difficult, it also has implications for collaborative teams of researchers, because of the need to reconcile political and value differences among them. In either case, the values and politics affect the choice of techniques as well as details of how they are used. They also constrain the choice of methodologies, such as action research, ethnography and philosophical research. Finally, and obviously, values and politics affect the researchers' stances to their chosen methodologies, stances which might be described, for instance, as 'feminist-postcolonial', 'critical-poststructuralist' or 'feminist-postmodernist'.

Taking an explicit stance helps to reduce bias, unless the stance is one of neutrality. The distinction between 'methodologies' and 'stances' can be illustrated by the observation that all three of the methodologies I mentioned in the previous paragraph, action research, ethnography and philosophical research, are represented as neutral by some researchers. On the other hand, it is precisely these methodologies which are the ones adopted by Melanie Walker, Stephen Ball and myself, but with explicit stances of feminist-postcolonial, critical-poststructuralist and feminist-postmodernist.[4] These are stances which have differences with each other, but none of them excludes the others. Each of them states its perspectives, so that a reader is able to judge how to take them into account in assessing the knowledge they produce. The stance of neutrality is different. Unlike other stances, it claims that it is the only possible representation of truth and knowledge, just because it is (it claims) neutral. But bias comes precisely from that representation, because it has the effect of hiding, not eliminating, partiality. The general point was made in Part II. It has also been argued for the particular cases of action research (Weiner 1989), ethnography (Altheide and Johnson 1994) and educational philosophical research (Martin 1994).

Bias in the wider context of educational research

Questions about the quality of research are not exhausted by giving satisfactory answers to questions about whether the research has been carried out well, using the principles of social justice in making decisions about the use of techniques and methodologies. There are also questions related to power-knowledge: questions of the effects of the way research is funded and used, and the meanings that are attached to its results. The structure of the system for doing research is a result of historical, social and economic circumstances, which includes the results and meanings attached to earlier research projects. In the case of England, the obvious influences are, currently, the bodies that fund it (e.g. QCA, TTA, HEFCE, ESRC, charities, industry), who gets to do it (e.g. teachers, LEAs, lecturers, contract researchers) and the ways in which it is directed (e.g. acceptability to a PhD supervisor or to a funding body). The kinds of research that result from this set of circumstances then reinforce or change the context, in their turn, in an endless feedback spiral. Dealing with this context is largely beyond the power of individual researchers in relation to their own projects. However, there is some value in reflexivity and adjustment. There is also something that can be done, collectively, at the level of the educational research community as a whole. I say more about this in Chapter 10.

Some ethical dilemmas

Ethical issues cannot be avoided in research (see Chapter 3), and there are plenty of discussions about it in general books on research (Robson 1993; Denzin and Lincoln 1994; Hitchcock and Hughes 1995). There exist a number of various sets of ethical guidelines issued by professional bodies, including the British Educational Research Association. The ten principles for social justice are themselves a set of guidelines with ethical implications. A view of ethics underpins them (see Chapter 5, pages 71–9), and taken together they form a basis for making ethical judgements. Underpinning the principles is: an equal respect for and appreciation of every individual; a recognition that persons are constructed and interpret themselves in relation to power relations in society, and they have real choices about how to do this; and an understanding that there are no hard and fast rules or certainties to be had, so moral decisions are always judgements in particular contexts. The principles highlight some ethical issues that are especially significant in research for social justice. These are related to: the quest for uncertain knowledge and improvement, which is always open to revision, so ethical decisions are never taken once for all (principles 1–3, 9); the importance attached to collaboration and working with others (principles 4–5); and the need to work within, against and through existing power differentials (principles 6–8). These issues can only be resolved in specific circumstances, which is the reason why I have explained something of each one with examples.

The vexed questions of informed consent, and the justification of deception, are something which has particular resonance for research self-consciously rooted in principles of openness and justice. Since the process is rooted in a willingness to reconsider and revise earlier decisions, such questions have to be revisited regularly, and judgements made and remade. To some extent, this is always going to be true for research processes which depend on participant observation, interviews, classroom-based action research or any other method which involves forming and keeping human relationships (Clandinin and Connelly 1994; Morse 1994; Punch 1994; Hitchcock and Hughes 1995).

The issue is sharpened in the case of social justice research, where it is precisely the effects of the justice of the relationship between the participants and the researchers which constitute some of the data. Ghazala Bhatti found herself in such a situation during her ethnographic research in a school (Bhatti 1995). The teachers 'knew', because it had been made clear to them at the outset of the research, that she was a qualified and experienced teacher. However, over the period of some years they forgot this, apparently seeing her as an Asian helper, who could be asked to run errands. One of them kindly told her that she might get a teaching qualification if she worked hard. She faced the issue of reminding them that she was not only a teacher, but also carrying out research for a doctorate. She herself raises this as a serious ethical issue with no obvious 'right' answer. If she had reminded them of her status, it is likely that they would have been far more likely to practise deception about their own views and behaviour with regard to ethnicity and education. Moreover, this evolving misperception of her was rightly treated as evidence to be analysed in relation to her research. (See also Neal (1995), who considers the dilemmas of research with 'an upward gaze'.)

The issue is sharpened when a researcher would not be able to explain their whole agenda at the beginning, because it would need some trust for it to be broached at all. When I began researching with Carol Davies in her classroom, she knew I was interested in equal opportunities, and was happy with that. It was only much later that we knew each other well enough to talk openly about questions related to teacher racism or sexuality (Griffiths and Davies 1995). I was never in a position in which I could have openly asked for her consent to do this. By the time we knew each other well enough, it would have been inappropriate to do so. In the event, the ethical issue was not a difficult one to resolve, because we were comfortable with the attitudes and behaviour of each other. It would have posed far more problems if I had been working with a teacher whom I felt had unacceptable attitudes. In those circumstances, even if I had agreed not to work explicitly in the controversial areas, I could not have pretended not to have evidence – which I would have almost certainly used in some anonymized form.

This issue of when to be open about what is also raised when someone is working as a change agent in a school to improve justice, and at the same time researching the process. For instance, Debbie Epstein's research was in primary schools in relation to gender and race (Epstein 1993). Like me, she could never have been in a position to obtain full consent from the beginning, even though she obtained consent in general. Like me, she was working in an under-researched area. It is my judgement that in these cases the importance of improving justice for children (and parents) in this area outweighs any absolute rights of informed consent for teachers, though within a general commitment to the normal research ethics in relation to collaboration. For instance, such principles would dictate that research should be reported sensitively, and discussed reasonably openly. At the least, participants retain their rights to anonymity, even if in some cases this means that details (for instance, names, places, dates) of the research report are fiction. In a similar kind of situation, Riddell discusses how she might best have handled the men and boys in her gender research so that collaborative principles would have been better upheld. Her useful reflection on this is entirely in keeping with principles 2 and 9, which look for improvements, not perfection:

> Once the research is underway, issues of honesty in field relations are constantly encountered . . . In disseminating the findings, a feminist researcher has to make difficult judgements between what will be acceptable to those who have provided the data [men and women], and the need of a wider audience to hear the whole story. Having collected and interpreted the data as sensitively as possible, I have taken upon myself responsibility for its publication . . . My own research would have been truer to feminist principles if it had been more of a collaborative process . . . If I ever embark on another ethnographic research project, I would like to spend longer thinking about how such collaboration can be achieved right from the start. Ultimately, the ethics of feminist research demand that the work should be useful to women.
>
> (Riddell 1989: 96–7)

Collaboration, reflexivity and power produce their own problems in relation to social justice. Reflexivity and collaboration imply openness, but this, like everything else, is not an absolute value. The ethical issue of respondents saying more than they mean, to the point of risking hurt from their self-exposure, is a recurring theme in qualitative research (Bridges 1989; Ball 1991; Paechter 1998; and see Chapter 3). Again, this issue is sharpened in research for social justice, precisely because unjust power relations mean that there are people who are at serious risk of having their personal or professional lives upset. One issue is the danger of being 'outed' by well meaning researchers. Obviously, this refers to lesbian or gay people, but it can also refer to other 'invisible' factors, of, say, disability, social class or even (non-visible) race. This is not just a matter of confidentiality and anonymity, but also of not putting people into positions where they reveal things they may not want to reveal about their identity. A colleague tells a story of being part of a research team in which one member, thinking to start with reflexive honesty, suggested that each person introduced themselves, and then described herself as an Anglo-Saxon, heterosexual, working-class woman. Some other members of the team were dismayed to find themselves under pressure to reveal aspects of their personal and medical histories or their sexuality – or to lie about them – when they had already gone to some lengths to conceal them, at least in professional settings.

Insider-outsiders

So far, this chapter has been about themes of bias and ethics, themes which are familiar to mainstream researchers. The questions of 'insider-outsider' perspectives are also discussed in the mainstream literature.[5] However, the discussions from the point of view of research for social justice might be said to be a kind of mirror image or Foucauldian 'reverse discourse' of the mainstream (Foucault 1979) on the subject of bias – although it is not usually carried out in terms of the word 'bias'.[6] There is, on the one hand, the claim that research from outsiders will be biased – and the reverse charge that research from insiders will be biased. On the other, there is the charge that insiders may have gone over to the academy, and become biased themselves, in that they have taken on its values, attitudes and beliefs to the extent that they are no longer true insiders. It is useful, therefore, to look at what might be implied by being an 'insider' or 'outsider': what it might mean to research your own community or to research as an outsider to a community. My argument is that no one in educational research is a complete insider or outsider. However, it is possible to recognize that some people are relative insiders or outsiders, in specific research contexts.

It is easy to talk about 'communities' and their 'insiders', but it is much harder to identify them. Being an insider or outsider might simply mean being black or white, female or male, middle class or working class, disabled or not. All these categories are themselves heterogeneous (see Part II, especially Chapter 5, pages 80–3). Michele Foster's (1994) discussion of insider research is structured around the distance to be spanned between highly educated black people and the communities they may have grown up in (see also hooks 1989; West 1993). Sewell's (1996b) discussion of his own role in Black masculine research draws on Collins's concept of the 'outsider-within': the black feminist within the academy but an outsider to it. Instead of just using the broad categories of 'black' or 'male', he analyses his response to a range of ways – conformists, rebels, innovators – in which black boys behaved in Township School:

> In this analysis of the data my insider status was confirmed when I heard my own voice in those of the children. My greatest sympathy went to the Conformists who were always in danger from the wrath of the peer group when they worked hard. My own experience of schooling often placed me in 'opposition' to what were prevailing 'Black peer group values'.

This kind of complex identification is also described by Walkerdine (1990: 157–8), reflecting on being 'a working-class girl who became a teacher and then an academic':

> Just as it is argued that there is not one black struggle but many black struggles, so the struggles of class are many, varied and full of contradictions . . . In 'Video Replay' I describe what happened when . . . I went into the home of a white working-class family to conduct some research. Where and who was I: the working-class child of my fantasies, or the middle-class researcher who was part of an attempt to tell a truth about 'The Working Class'?

Similarly, Mehreen Mirza analyses the ways in which she was like, and also unlike, her research informants (see Chapters 2 and 3). Kaye Haw's (1998) research on Muslim girls brings out a different set of ways in which researchers have to negotiate a complex set of insider-outsider identifications. Her research is into the schooling of Asian Muslim girls in England. As she points out, she is partly an outsider (white, non-believing but of Christian heritage) and partly an insider (female, ex-teacher, British). In reflexive response to such complexity, her book has contributions from a researcher with a different set of insider-outsider identifications (Pakistani-Muslim, a teacher, brought up and working in Pakistan).

Relative insiders have to face the charge that they are too distanced from the community which they have researched: that they might have become empowered themselves, and found a voice, but that this should not be confused with the voice of other people in that community. But to say this is to present only two possibilities. There are others. I quoted Michele Foster in Chapter 8, first carefully and clearly differentiating the different voices in the black communities she studied, and also her own; second, explaining the importance of having these voices, including her own, as a counterweight to the stereotypes of the dominant discourse. Sewell (1996b) argues that he, too, has achieved a similar range of aims, particularly since he has presented and discussed the research not only in his academic community, but also in Township and similar schools, replaying the boys' voices to them and using them to continue the dialogue. Relative insiders have to face the question of having sold out to the norms and forms of most educational research. There are, of course, no easy answers here, as the earlier quotation from Walkerdine indicates. She suggests one:

> I call myself an 'educated working-class woman' . . . This may be a fictional identity like all the others, but it allows something to be spoken and some things to come together: educated, working-class and woman – three terms which I thought were hopelessly fragmented. Terms which assert my education and my power with pride and claim back my education, not as alienation and a move to another class but as part of a narrative which allows me a place from which to struggle, a sense of belonging.
>
> (Walkerdine 1990: 158)

Individuals all have to make up their own narratives, many of which can be found in the kind of autobiographical and/or reflexive accounts I have been using. How far such reflexivity can be judged to be successful is another matter, and I say some more about this in the next chapter.

'Selling out' is a kind of hypocrisy. Charges of hypocrisy are also levelled at relative outsiders, who are in danger of exploiting the communities where they research, and even making things worse by strengthening the stereotypes (see Chapter 8). Relative outsiders can respond to such charges with a reflexivity about their lives as a whole, the actions that they take as well as the research that they do, both in and out of academic life (Fine 1994). To say this is merely to point to the conclusions of the book so far with respect to collaboration, empowerment and the struggle for justice. Thus, for instance, the use of 'voice' needs to be negotiated and renegotiated with those whose voice it supposedly is. For instance, do they need or want space to come to a voice? Or do they, perhaps, only need the researcher as a kind of megaphone with which to talk to those they need to influence? What kind of reciprocity has been offered? How is the research coherent with the decisions made about whom to support and whose views to respect? The issue of reflexivity is considered further in the next chapter.

Notes

1 Some books escape this criticism. Denzin and Lincoln's (1994) handbook is good; so is Hitchcock and Hughes (1995). But otherwise useful books like Cohen and Manion (1989), Robson (1993) and Morse (1994) appear hardly to notice the issues.
2 Research method books are good sources for the various kinds of data, analysis, reporting, validity and reliability aimed at. Again (see previous note), Denzin and Lincoln (1994) and Hitchcock and Hughes (1995) are good sources of principles of procedure and pitfalls to be avoided.
3 See also the debate between Wright and Foster, which raised the question of how much weight to put on the perspectives of black children relative to white teachers. This is still an argument within the academic community. Hitchcock and Hughes (1995: 107) argue that Foster was only raising this question, not answering it, but see Chapter 4, where I suggest a different interpretation, drawing on Connolly (1992).
4 I said '*might* be described' earlier because I am well aware how these terms are rough categorizations, threatening to pigeon hole researchers in a way they would resist. Indeed, I have applied one of these terms to me, and I am already inclined to resist it!
5 Sometimes in terms which oppose 'emic, idiographic' to 'etic, nomothetic' (e.g. Morse 1994; Denzin and Lincoln 1995).
6 Riddell (1989: 92) reviews evidence that bias is alleged only when the researcher takes the perspective of the subordinate group in a hierarchical relationship.

10 | Educational research at large

Reflexivity

Reflexivity and responsibilities

Of the set of ten 'principles for social justice in educational research', there are two (principles 7 and 8) which depend on the word 'reflexivity'. Reflexivity is implied in the set as a whole. However, these two were put in to emphasize the responsibility of researchers for their own practices, in spite of the strength of the constraints of their personal history and social-political context. Anyway, as explained earlier, the principles have to be understood as a whole: the earlier ones frame the later ones and the later ones explain the earlier ones. In some accounts of reflexivity in research (e.g. Siraj-Blatchford and Siraj-Blatchford 1997), acting on the other principles constitutes reflexivity: paying attention to the view points of the subjects of research; and collaborating as far as possible (consonant with the other principles) at all stages, including design, analysis and dissemination. Reflexivity provides a way of acting on the knowledge that knowledge is perspectival and on the possibility that there may be a complete change of mind in the middle: that is, acting on the view that 'All knowledge and claims to knowledge are reflexive of the process, assumptions, location, history, and context of knowing and the knower' (Altheide and Johnson 1994: 488). In other accounts, there is a further emphasis: reflexivity is also about 'relations to oneself' in the process of research (Elliott 1991b; Gore 1993). An important aspect of this from the point of view of research for social justice is, as Troyna argued, our relationship with our selves as politically positioned and politically active (Riddell and Vincent 1997).

It is all very well advocating reflexivity, but it is not a straightforward business. Researchers need to have some clarity about what kinds of responsibility can be exercised as individuals and as collectives. No one is responsible for everything. Some things have to be done with others: here I am thinking particularly of the wider educational research community. Others can be done by individuals with their immediate research team or collaborative group. Principle 9 (there is no hope of doing perfect research) is particularly important here: reflexivity is based on the view that perfection is never possible, although improvement always is. For instance, collaboration may be desirable for reflexivity to work, but it is not always possible. Some research is done on the run. Some is designed by others. Sometimes all three are true: the research has to hide its collaborative face, be done on the run *and* work within a method designed by others. The research by David Gillborn and Caroline Gipps (1996) appears to be like this. It had to be done within the given framework, which does not appear to be that of the researchers, but they judged that it was worth doing even so. (I think they were right.) This section looks at the possibilities and pitfalls of reflexivity for individuals and teams, and the next one at the educational research community as a whole.

Possibilities and pitfalls of reflexivity for individual researchers and research teams

We in the West live in a social context that puts great store on the individuality and agency of individuals. It is tempting to imagine that reflexivity makes it possible to escape from ourselves, and to find a new, safe position that escapes our own positionality. It is also tempting to imagine that through being reflexive we can see where to act most effectively, and then do so. I have described these as temptations, because they lead a researcher away from the hard, unremitting work of reflexivity, the work which is implicit in principles 3 and 9: 'all improvements and knowledge are uncertain' and 'there is no hope of doing perfect research'. Reflexivity is a difficult and continuing process, with a constant likelihood of getting things wrong and having to put them right again. In relation to ourselves and our own actions, it is also about achieving and re-achieving our own authenticity.[1]

Faced with these difficulties, it is all too easy not to get started at all. This is, of course, no solution. It may be easy, especially in some academic contexts, simply to carry on reflecting. However, this is self-defeating as a strategy. If the research is not under way, and the researchers are not actively engaged, they will be unable to access the points of view and perspectives of others. You have to start somewhere, and wherever that is it will be subject to more reflection. The discussion of Mac an Ghaill's work in Chapter 8, shows how necessary it was for the research to be in process, in order that the perspectives of students – and other educational researchers – could change its direction.

Another strategy, though a hypocritical one, for dealing with the difficulties is to give the appearance of reflection, but without any accompanying actions.

(Compare the charges of hypocrisy noted at the end of Chapter 9.) On the one hand, there are the seductions of autobiography and self-gaze. Writing about the self can become an end in itself. It can also become an exercise in self-justification, drawing on the Western autobiographical tradition of writing the self as hero – even if she is sometimes a tragic hero. I agree with Patai (1994), who argues that this is a problem – though I disagree with her suggested solution of leaving such self-analysis out of research and scholarship altogether. I have been arguing that reflexivity demands an attention to biography as part of an honest dialogue about 'forces of difference, divergence and contradiction' (Fine 1994: 31).[2] On the other hand, it is not hard to put in the apparent performance of reflexivity by a series of cosmetic moves. There are plenty of examples: an announcement of a position such as 'male', 'female', 'gay', 'lesbian', 'heterosexual', as if that indicated, in itself, a reflexive positionality; an announcement that research is 'feminist' or 'anti-racist', without any engagement with either theory or practice in the area; a use of both 'he' and 'she' as generic pronouns, – but thinking 'he'; commarization – the addition of lists, like race, class, gender – without that making any difference to the project in hand. Les Back (1996: 23) describes this last ploy, particularly in relation to working-class culture, as 'radical credentialism': 'It seems to me that such rhetorical moves are little more than micro-political gestures determined by the politics of the academy'.

Intellectual tourism is more self-deceiving than hypocritical. It is an understandable response to the wide variety of perspectives, the pace and intensification of change and the ever increasing explosion of knowledge (see Part II, especially Chapter 5, pages 80–3). Nobody can listen to all the relevant voices and read all the relevant books. Some people respond to this as if they were tourists faced with a world of difference. Tourists traditionally take photographs and fill their houses with souvenirs, but they do not come back seriously changed by the experience of travel. Similarly, intellectual and cultural tourists can cherry-pick names and quotations, but do not have their own perspectives challenged. And, as mentioned in Chapter 8, pages 124–8, they can use the voices of the subjects of research to prop up a framework rather than challenge it. But as always, there is no perfection to be had (principle 9). A lot of travelling is bound to be tourism, and I don't think we should all stay at home (Seller 1994; Haw 1996). A commitment to continuing reflexivity will bring about a more ethical tourism, in which the impossibility of attending to all perspectives is recognized, without that being a licence to attend to none.[3]

Reflexivity at large: the educational research community

I have been addressing individual research within a framework which emphasizes how context-bound any researcher is. Some of that context is, precisely, the educational research community as a whole. All educational researchers are members of this community, and in acknowledging it, have some room for manoeuvre within it. This is important because of the influence this context has on the possibilities of working for social justice. Principle 10 deals with emphasizing the significance of the observation that as educational researchers we are all members of this community and can choose to acknowledge it.

Space would be made for getting more justice in educational research if there were more formal acknowledgement of the effects of the taken-for-granted processes within the educational research community. These effects may be informally obvious, but they are hardly ever discussed formally as affecting the research process. This reticence is in stark contrast to the enthusiastic circulation of anecdote about, for instance, hunting for grants, how to deal with difficult supervisors or students and rumours about the Research Assessment Exercises[4], and who is doing what in response. In previous chapters, especially Chapters 7 and 9, I argued that the context in which the research is done is at least as influential on the course of the research as anything an individual could decide about the processes of their research. Yet formal accounts of research hardly ever acknowledge these influences, nor do most research methods books (though see Punch 1994).

The lack of attention to the combined effect of such constraints probably occurs because their *systematic* significance for the nature of research gets missed. Yet it is not hard to see that the systematic working out of apparent accidentals in the resolution of dilemmas related to working with the constraints has implications for social justice: a kind of 'institutional injustice' by analogy with institutional sexism or racism. There are plenty of indications that this is happening. Witness the continuing complaints of women and black people about supervision and funding. And witness the socio-political bias in who get to be gatekeepers, to be on editorial boards, funding councils or charity boards. The few examples of reflexive discussions of such factors are very useful. Action research is one arena where they occur, though mainly in relation to teachers and academics, rather than other imbalances of power. I referred to one of these discussions in Chapter 8 (Gitlin and Russell 1994). Some of the effects of the involvement of higher education in teacher research in Britain are discussed by Somekh (1995) and, less optimistically, by MacLure (1996). Siraj-Blatchford (1994: 11) discusses the effect of funders' views of valid research and the likelihood that a positivist approach would be favoured by them, though less so by much of the academic world. Donald *et al.* (1995) discuss the effect of available funding on research design in relation to the funders' perceptions of the kinds of problems that need solving. Stephen Ball reflects on the context of policy research and how, even if critical researchers are 'apparently safely ensconced in the moral high ground', policy research is always in some degree 'both reactive and parasitic' on the prevailing and changing moral economy (Ball 1997: 258).

If there is a problem of institutional injustices, then it is the responsibility of educational researchers to start to redress them. More reflexivity is needed in the educational community as a whole. On the one hand, this is a matter of working with those who are influential in the community but who think that good intentions are enough – but without alarming them unduly. They need to be shaken into reflexivity. On the other hand, there is a need for researchers for social justice to work together and to support each other, by developing structures which facilitate communication between them and then using these structures to exchange perspectives and strategies.

I am not advocating a grand, rational plan. The 'principles for social justice in educational research' still apply. As with all strategies for justice, this is a matter of local action, and of operating through and between dominant discourses. Researchers can join large networks and engage in small collaborations. There needs to be a continuing interrogation of how any area of research fits into the larger context as the first stage in getting improvement. And then such improvement needs to be interrogated in its turn. Stephen Ball's examination of policy research, mentioned above, is one useful example. He concludes:

> There is a basic and apparently irredeemable tension at the heart of education policy research. A tension between the concerns of efficiency and those of social justice . . . Individual researchers must address, or try to resolve, the tension as they see fit; although it just may be that some of one side has to be sacrificed to achieve more of the other.
>
> (Ball 1997: 271)

Another example is provided by Brine's discussion of the question of European funding, in which she argues for the importance of an appreciation of the relevance, for social justice, of understanding European funding structures, in order to seek out the possibilities of finding ways of working for social justice:

> A European Union is being constructed . . . European-funded research is part of this construction . . . This has presented definite possibilities for cross-European social justice research, and networks have been formed of researchers focusing on migrants, on women, on people with disabilities, and on many aspects of poverty and social exclusion.
>
> (Brine 1997: 431–2)

Patchy research

Educational research for social justice, as I have described it in this book, seems to be a patchwork of big and little pieces of research carried out by a very wide range of people. In the course of the book, I have mentioned some very large-scale projects: policy research in Europe; research that has been highly influential on government policy; well funded research that has spanned years; and very well known research that has helped to change the course of thinking in some area of education. On the other hand, I have also mentioned much smaller-scale research, aimed at single classrooms, for instance, or directly relevant only to a few schools in a single LEA. Some of this small-scale work is published, but only in the sense that those most closely involved have reports – some of which have been verbal.

This is as it should be. There is no one right way to carry out research for social justice. Moreover, work has to go on in a number of arenas simultaneously. None is prior to another. What is needed is an attitude of 'both/and' rather than 'either/or'. This has been a continuing theme of this book, more abstractly in Part II, more concretely in Part III, and also in the choice of examples all the way through. There are two consequences for educational researchers – and for the communities in which they work. First, it is important to work your own patch without pouring scorn on others. The rich variety of ways of researching for social justice can and should lead to critical exchanges; this does not imply that one kind of work is superior to another. Everything depends on opportunity and context. Second, the patches overlap in an indefinite number of ways. This means that work in one can learn from work in another. It also means that each patch can be used in more than one way. To put this another way, there is more than one kind of story to be told from a single research project or set of projects. David Gillborn and Caroline Gipps's review of achievement research is a clear example. They presented the research in one form, which is the one I have discussed here. It has also featured in other forms, more critical and reflexive, for other purposes (see, for instance, Gillborn 1997). Melanie Walker's research is another example. It has been presented in different ways: as a PhD thesis, to the teachers with whom she worked and in a series of reflective articles, of which the article discussed here is one (see also Walker 1996a, b).

It is worth noting here that both these pieces of research draw on local knowledge, marked by the values of the researchers, but are proposed as useful on a larger scale. David Gillborn and Caroline Gipps make use of a number of small-scale projects to inform government policy in the whole country, although they were originally presented, reflexively, as the work of particular researchers. Melanie Walker suggests how to join patches together into whole cloth:

> I believe that a theoretically informed action research is one way forward towards a different construction of teachers (in schools and universities) as flexible, critical and reflective practitioners able to develop quality education and realise core values of equity and social justice. Such action research would challenge hegemonic voices or traditions

which gloss over the different, multiple and competing voices . . . For me then, change, development and understanding . . . lie in shifting from common sense to good sense, but in ways which recognise that the common does not exclude the good and the good can be fashioned out of the common.

A political strategy for educational research for social justice is not to be found in any one methodology or in any overarching grand plan. There is no need for a clarion call to unite all the disparate strands and interests into a single, unified movement. There is no reason to level out difference, spontancity and the fun of individual creativity in the interests of large-scale uniformity. Rather, the political strategy is one which requires each of us to reassess our own options and opportunities at the same time that we take a shrewd, critical view of the larger context which gave rise to them. Social justice is for the good of individuals and of their communities: therefore, it has to be for our own personal good and for the good of our own communities, too. In other words, the strategy is to do what you can, and to keep your wits about you, and your ears open, and still be able to live with yourself.

Notes

1 I say more about the continuing process of achieving authenticity in my book on the self (Griffiths 1995a).
2 The articles by Patai and Fine are part of a three-way dialogue with Patti Lather about power and method in feminist research.
3 I say some more about the process of selective attention and cultural tourism in my book on the self (Griffiths 1995a).
4 British universities are subject to regular 'research assessment exercises'. Universities submit evidence of their research activity and quality to a series of national panels. These submissions are then assessed and rank ordered. The rank is used to determine levels of research funding for each university.

Appendix: Fair schools

1 *A fair school is always a learning community of pupils, teachers, support staff, parents and neighbourhood.*
   'Equality is not the end but the way.' The same is true for fairness.

2 *A condition for the establishment of a learning community is the valuing of everybody in conditions of trust and safety.*
   These conditions take time to establish. People can only learn from the continuing actions of others that they can give their trust. And they can only learn from the continuing actions that they are both valued and safe.

3 *Learning requires being wholeheartedly consultative of everybody in the community, open and able to deal with change.*
   Being wholehearted means not being cynical about actions. Consulting everybody means consulting with all those affected by the school, both inside and out of it: both home and community, and with pupils, teachers and support staff.

4 *It is acknowledged that consultation and change are going to result in some conflict and people feeling exposed when putting their views on the line.*
   The process of accommodating the views of everybody feels risky. So everybody, whether headteacher or first-year pupil, has to feel safe about expressing themselves. They also have to be willing to find that others do not agree with their perspectives.

5 *There is an in-built chance of learning leading to a complete change of direction (including of dearly held values and traditions).*
   A change of direction means wholeheartedly holding the new values. This cannot be undertaken lightly. The point is to acknowledge that people can change their minds when they learn.

6 *Meanwhile, it is important that both the leadership and also the rest of the school has a clear ethos and tries to act on it.*
   The core values must be the ones that create conditions for learning. The ethos must support this.

7 *Instant utopia is not to be found – fairness has to be constructed on the run.*
   By the time the best solution is found for certain, the situation will have changed. It's important to do what you can, now, rather than wait until it is better planned out.

8 *Utopia is not to be found.*
   A fair school still needs to improve. It's important to start from where the school is, improving what it has. This may mean that there are areas in which a school is excellent, even while it needs to work hard on other areas, and even while some other things may be out of its control altogether.

9 *Improvements always come as a patchwork or ragbag.*
   There can never be a tidy overarching rationale or masterplan for improving fairness. Events move too fast.

10 *Improvements in fairness need to be recognized and celebrated.*
   It is important not to be weighed down by all the things that remain to be done. Working for fairness is already to be doing the most important thing.

11 *Consultation means that the school undergoes a constant process of review and revision.*
   But don't try to deal with everything at once: change the focus of attention.

12 *Alliances between different interest groups need to be supported at the same time as all the different groups are acknowledged and valued.*
   There are alliances to be made between groups of people on the basis of, for example, class, race, gender, social class and sexuality. They cross-cut alliances between, for example, teachers, advisors, children and parents. All these groups need acknowledgement, support and understanding.

References

Altheide, David L. and Johnson, John M. (1994) Criteria for assessing interpretive validity in qualitative research. In Norman K. Denzin and Yvonna S. Lincoln (eds) *Handbook of Qualitative Research*. London: Sage.

Aristotle (1980) *The Nicomachean Ethics*. Oxford: Oxford University Press.

Aristotle (1995) *Politics*. Oxford: Oxford University Press.

Askew, Sue and Ross, Carol (1988) *Boys Don't Cry*. Milton Keynes: Open University Press.

Back, Les (1996) *New Ethnicities and Urban Culture: Racisms and Multiculture in Young Lives*. London: UCL Press.

Ball, Stephen (1987) *The Micro-politics of the School: towards a Theory of School Organization*. London: Routledge.

Ball, Stephen (1990) *Politics and Policy Making in Education*. London: Routledge.

Ball, Stephen (1991) Power, conflict, micropolitics and all that! In Geoffrey Walford (ed.) *Doing Educational Research*. London: Routledge.

Ball, Stephen (1994) *Education Reform: a Critical and Post-structural Approach*. Buckingham: Open University Press.

Ball, Stephen (1997) Policy sociology and critical social research: a personal review of recent education policy and policy research, *British Educational Research Journal*, 23(3), 257–74.

Bauman, Zygmunt (1993) *Postmodern Ethics*. Oxford: Blackwell.

Bell, Colin and Raffe, David (1991) Working together? Research, policy and practice. The experience of the Scottish evaluation of TVEI. In Geoffrey Walford (ed.) *Doing Educational Research*. London: Routledge.

Benhabib, Seyla (1992) *Situating the Self: Gender, Community and Postmodernism in Contemporary Ethics*. Cambridge: Polity Press.

Bhatti, Ghazala (1995) A journey into the unknown: an ethnographic study of Asian children. In Morwenna Griffiths and Barry Troyna (eds) *Antiracism, Culture and Social Justice in Education*. Stoke-on-Trent: Trentham Books.

Bhavani, Kum-Kum (1988) Empowerment and social research: some comments, *Text*, 8, 41–50.

Biddulph, Max (1996) Can only Dorothy's friends speak for Dorothy? Exploring issues of biographical positioning in qualitative research with gay/bisexual men.

Paper presented to British Educational Research Association Annual Conference, Lancaster University.

Bridges, David (1989) Ethics and the law: conducting case studies of policing. In Robert C. Burgess (ed.) *The Ethics of Educational Research*. London: Falmer Press.

Brine, Jacky (1997) Over the ditch and through the thorns: accessing European funds for research and social justice, *British Educational Research Journal*, 23(4), 421–32.

Broadfoot, Patricia (1988) Educational research: two cultures and three estates, *British Educational Research Journal*, 14(1), 3–16.

Brown, Sally (1991) Effective contributions from research to educational conversations: style and strategy, *British Educational Research Journal*, 17(1), 5–18.

Bryman, Alan (1988) *Quantity and Quality in Social Research*. London: Unwin Hyman.

Bryman, Alan and Burgess, Robert G. (1994) *Analysing Qualitative Data*. London: Routledge.

Carr, Wilfred (1997) Professing education in a postmodern age, *Journal of Philosophy of Education*, 31, 309–27.

Clandinin, D. Jean and Connelly, F. Michael (1994) Personal experience methods. In Norman K. Denzin and Yvonna S. Lincoln (eds) *Handbook of Qualitative Research*. London: Sage.

Coard, Bernard (1971) *How the West Indian Child Is Made Educationally Subnormal in the British School System*. London: New Beacon.

Cockburn, Cynthia (1989) Equal opportunities: the short and long agenda, *Industrial Relations Journal*, Autumn, 213–25.

Cockburn, Cynthia (1991) *In the Way of Women: Men's Resistance to Sex Equality in Organizations*. London: Macmillan.

Cohen, Louis and Manion, Lawrence (1989) *Research Methods in Education*. London: Routledge.

Collins, Patricia Hill (1990) *Black Feminist Thought*. London: Routledge.

Commission for Social Justice (1993) *The Justice Gap*. London: Institute for Public Policy Research.

Connolly, Paul (1992) Playing it by the rules: the politics of research in 'race' and education, *British Educational Research Journal*, 18(2), 133–48.

Cordingly, Philippa (1996) Teachers and research: the TTA's role in bridging the gap, *Research Intelligence*, 58, 10–11.

Davies, Bronwen (1989) *Frogs and Snails and Feminist Tales: Preschool Children and Gender*. Sydney: Allen and Unwin.

Delamont, Sara (1992) *Fieldwork in Educational Settings: Methods, Pitfalls and Perspectives*. London: Falmer Press.

Denzin, Norman K. and Lincoln, Yvonna S. (eds) (1994) *Handbook of Qualitative Research*. London: Sage.

Dewey, John (1916) *Democracy and Education*. Toronto: Collier Macmillan.

Dey, Ian (1993) *Qualitative Data Analysis*. London: Routledge.

Donald, Patricia, Gosling, Susan, Hamilton, Jean, Hawkes, Nicholas, McKenzie, David and Stronach, Ian (1995) 'No problem here': action research against racism in a mainly white area, *British Educational Research Journal*, 21(3), 263–75.

Elbaz, Robert (1988) *The Changing Nature of the Self*. London: Croom Helm.

Elliott, John (1990) Educational research in crisis: performance indicators and the decline in excellence, *British Educational Research Journal*, 16(1), 3–18.

Elliott, John (1991) *Action Research for Educational Change*. Milton Keynes: Open University Press.

Elliott, John (1996) Quality assurance, the educational standards debate, and the commodification of educational research. Paper presented to British Educational Research Association Annual Conference, Lancaster University.

Epstein, Debbie (1993) *Changing Classroom Cultures: Anti-racism, Politics and Schools*. Stoke-on-Trent: Trentham Books.

Epstein, Debbie (ed.) (1994) *Challenging Lesbian and Gay Inequalities in Education*. Buckingham: Open University Press.

Epstein, Debbie and Johnson, Richard (1994) On the straight and narrow: the heterosexual presumption, homophobias and schools. In Debbie Epstein (ed.), *Challenging Lesbian and Gay Inequalities in Education*. Buckingham: Open University Press.

Evans, Mary (ed.) (1982) *The Woman Question: Readings on the Subordination of Women*. Oxford: Fontana.

Fanon, Frantz (1952) *Black Skin, White Masks*. London: Pluto Press.

Fine, Michelle (1994) Dis-stance and other stances: negotiations of power inside feminist research. In Andrew Gitlin (ed.) *Power and Method: Political Activism and Educational Research*. London: Routledge.

Floud, J. E. and Halsey, A. H. (1957) Intelligence tests, social class and selection for secondary schools, *British Journal of Sociology*, 8.

Fonow, Mary and Cook, Judith (eds) (1991) *Beyond Methodology: Feminist Scholarship as Lived Research*. Bloomington: Indiana University Press.

Foster, Michèle (1994) The power to know one thing is never the power to know all things: methodological notes on two studies of Black American teachers. In Andrew Gitlin (ed.) *Power and Method: Political Activism and Educational Research*. London: Routledge.

Foster, Peter (1990a) *Policy and Practice in Multicultural and Anti-racist Education*. London: Routledge.

Foster, Peter (1990b) Cases not proven: an evaluation of two studies of teacher racism, *British Educational Research Journal*, 16(4), 334–49.

Foster, Peter (1991) Case still not proven: a reply to Cecile Wright, *British Educational Research Journal*, 17(2), 165–70.

Foster, Peter (1992) What are Connolly's Rules?, *British Educational Research Journal*, 18(2), 149–54.

Foster, Peter and Hammersley, Martyn (1996) Researching educational inequality: a critique, *Research Intelligence*, 56, 18–20.

Foucault, Michel (1979) *The History of Sexuality: an Introduction*. Harmondsworth: Penguin.

Foucault, Michel (1980) *Power/Knowledge: Selected Interviews and Other Writings*. London: Harvester Wheatsheaf.

Foucault, Michel (1984) What is Enlightenment? In Paul Rabinow (ed.) *The Foucault Reader*. Harmondsworth: Penguin.

Foucault, Michel (1988) The ethic of care for the self as a practice of freedom: an interview. In James Bernauer and David Rasmussen (eds) *The Final Foucault*. London: MIT Press.

Freire, Paulo (1972) *Pedagogy of the Oppressed*. Harmondsworth: Penguin.

Gillborn, David (1990) *'Race', Ethnicity and Education: Teaching and Learning in Multi-ethnic Schools*. London: Unwin Hyman.

Gillborn, David (1995) *Racism and Antiracism in Real Schools*. Buckingham: Open University Press.

Gillborn, David (1997) Racism and reform: new ethnicities/old inequalities?, *British Educational Research Journal*, 23(3), 345–60.

Gillborn, David and Gipps, Caroline (1996) *Recent Research on the Achievements of Ethnic Minority Pupils*. London: HMSO (Ofsted).

Gilroy, Paul (1993) *The Black Atlantic: Modernity and Double Consciousness*. London: Verso.

Gipps, Caroline (1993) The profession of educational research, *British Educational Research Journal*, 19(1), 3–16.

Gipps, Caroline and Murphy, Patricia (1994) *A Fair Test? Assessment, Achievement and Equity*. Buckingham: Open University Press.

Gitlin, Andrew and Russell, Robyn (1994) Alternative methodologies and the research context. In Andrew Gitlin (ed.) *Power and Method: Political Activism and Educational Research*. London: Routledge.

Gore, Jennifer (1993) *The Struggle for Pedagogies: Critical and Feminist Discourses as Regimes of Truth*. London: Routledge.

Gore, Jennifer (1997) On the use of empirical research for the development of a theory of pedagogy, *Cambridge Journal of Education*, 27(2), 211–22.

Gramsci, Antonio (1971) *Selections from the Prison Notebooks*. London: Lawrence and Wishart.

Gray, John (1995) *Enlightenment's Wake: Politics and Culture at the Close of the Modern Age*. London: Routledge.

Gray, John, Goldstein, Harvey and Kay, William (1997) Educational research and research-based practice, *Research Intelligence*, 59, 18–20.

Griffiths, Morwenna (1987) The teaching of skills and the skills of teaching, *Journal of Philosophy of Education*, 21(2), 203–14.

Griffiths, Morwenna (1988) Strong feelings about computers, *Women's Studies International Forum 11*, 20, 145–54.

Griffiths, Morwenna (1995a) *Feminisms and the Self: the Web of Identity*. London: Routledge.

Griffiths, Morwenna (1995b) Making a difference: feminism, postmodernism and the methodology of educational research, *British Educational Research Journal*, 21(2), 219–35.

Griffiths, Morwenna (1998a) Aiming for a fair education: what use is philosophy? In R. Marples (ed.) *The Aims of Education*. London: Routledge.

Griffiths, Morwenna (1998b) The discourses of social justice in schools, *British Educational Research Journal*, 24(3), 301–16.

Griffiths, Morwenna and Alfrey, Margaret (1989) A stereotype in the making: girls and computers in primary schools, *Educational Review*, 41(1), 73–9.

Griffiths, Morwenna and Davies, Carol (1995) *In Fairness to Children: Working for Social Justice in the Primary School*. London: David Fulton.

Griffiths, Morwenna and Parker-Jenkins, Marie (1994) Methodological and ethical dilemmas in international research: school attendance and gender in Ghana, *Oxford Review of Education*, 20(4), 441–59.

Griffiths, Morwenna and Troyna, Barry (eds) (1995) *Antiracism, Culture and Social Justice in Education*. Stoke-on-Trent: Trentham.

Hamilton, David (1990) *Learning about Education: an Unfinished Curriculum*. Milton Keynes: Open University Press.

Hammersley, Martyn (1995) *The Politics of Social Research*. London: Sage.

Hammersley, Martyn (1997) Educational research and teaching: a response to David Hargreaves' TTA lecture, *British Educational Research Journal*, 23(2), 141–61.

Haraway, Donna J. (1991) *Simians, Cyborgs, and Women: the Reinvention of Nature*. London: Free Association Books.

Harding, Sandra (1988) Is there a feminist method? In Sandra Harding (ed.) *Feminism and Methodology: Social Science Issues*. Milton Keynes: Open University Press.

Harding, Sandra (1991) *Whose Science? Whose Knowledge? Thinking from Women's Lives*. Milton Keynes: Open University Press.

Hargreaves, Andy (1994) *Changing Teachers, Changing Times*. London: Cassell.

Hargreaves, David (1996) Teaching as a research-based profession: possibilities and prospects. Teacher Training Agency Annual Lecture.

Hargreaves, David (1997) Educational research and evidence-based educational practice – a response to critics, *Research Intelligence*, 58, 12–16.

Hastings, N. and Schwieso, J. J. (1995) Tasks and tables: the effect of seating arrangements on task engagement in primary classrooms, *Educational Research*, 37(3), 279–91.

Haw, Kaye F. (1996) Exploring the educational experiences of Muslim girls: tales told to tourists – should the white researcher stay at home?, *British Educational Research Journal*, 22(3), 319–30.

Haw, Kaye (1998) *Educating Muslim Girls: Shifting Discourses*. Buckingham: Open University Press.

Heisenberg, Werner (1971) *Physics and Beyond: Encounters and Conversations*. London: George Allen and Unwin.

Hitchcock, Graham and Hughes, David (1995) *Research and the Teacher: a Qualitative Introduction to School-based Research*, 2nd cdn. London: Routledge.

Hogan, Padraig (1995) *The Custody and Courtship of Experience. Western Education in Philosophical Perspective*. Dublin: Columba.

Honig, B. (1992) Toward an agonistic feminism: Hannah Arendt and the politics of identity. In Judith Butler and Joan W. Scott (eds) *Feminists Theorize the Political*. London: Routledge.

hooks, bell (1989) *Talking Back: Thinking Feminist, Thinking Black*. London: Sheba.

Hume, David (1739) *A Treatise of Human Nature: Book One*. Glasgow: Fontana/Collins.

Hume, David (1740) *A Treatise of Human Nature: Books Two and Three*. Glasgow: Fontana/Collins.

Hutchings, Kimberly (1995) *Kant, Critique and Politics*. London: Routledge.

Jackson, Brian and Marsden, Dennis (1962) *Education and the Working Class*. Harmondsworth: Penguin.

Jonathan, Ruth (1995) Liberal philosophy of education: a paradigm under strain, *Journal of Philosophy of Education*, 29(1), 93–107.

Kelly, Alison (1998) Education or Indoctrination? The ethics of school based action research. In Robert G. Burgess (ed.) *The Ethics of Educational Research*. London: Falmer 110–13.

Kierkegaard, Soren (1843) *Fear and Trembling*. Harmondsworth: Penguin.

Lacey, Colin (1970) *Hightown Grammar: the School as a Social System*. Manchester: Manchester University Press.

Ladson-Billings, Gloria (1994) *The Dreamkeepers: Successful Teaching for African-American Students*. San Francisco: Jossey Bass.

Lally, Vic and Scaife, Jon (1995) Towards a collaborative approach to teacher empowerment, *British Educational Research Journal*, 21(3), 323–38.

Lather, Patti (1988) Feminist perspectives on empowering research methodologies. In Janet Holland and Maud Blair (eds, 1995) *Debates and Issues in Feminist Research and Pedagogy*. Clevedon: Multilingual Matters.

Lather, Patti (1991) *Getting Smart: Feminist Research with/in the Postmodern*. London: Routledge.

Lather, Patti (1994) Fertile obsession: validity after poststructuralism. In Andrew Gitlin (ed.) *Power and Method: Political Activism and Educational Research*. London: Routledge.

Lawson, John and Silver, Harold (1973) *A Social History of Education in England*. London: Methuen.

Lawton, Denis (1977) *Education and Social Justice*. London: Sage.

Lennon, Kathleen and Whitford, Margaret (eds) (1994) *Knowing the Difference: Feminist Perspectives in Epistemology*. London: Routledge.

Lodge, Paul and Blackstone, Tessa (1982) *Educational Policy and Educational Inequality*. Oxford: Martin Robertson.

Lomax, Pamela (1991) Peer review and action research. In Pamela Lomax (ed.) *Managing Better Schools and Colleges: an Action Research Way*. Clevedon: Multilingual Matters.

Lorde, Audre (1984) *Sister Outsider*. New York: The Crossing Press.

Lukes, Steven (1974) *Power: a Radical View*. London: Macmillan.

Lyotard, Jean-François (1984) *The Postmodern Condition: a Report on Knowledge*. Manchester: Manchester University Press.

Lyotard, Jean-François (1992) *The Postmodern Explained to Children: Correspondence 1982–1985*. London: Turnaround.

Mac an Ghaill, Maírtín (1988) *Young, Gifted and Black: Student–Teacher Relations in the Schooling of Black Youth*. Milton Keynes: Open University Press.

Mac an Ghaill, Maírtín (1991) Young, gifted and black: methodological reflections of a teacher/researcher. In Geoffrey Walford (ed.) *Doing Educational Research*. London: Routledge.

Mac an Ghaill, Maírtín (1994) (In)visibility: sexuality, race and masculinity in the school context. In Debbie Epstein (ed.) *Challenging Lesbian and Gay Inequalities in Education*. Buckingham: Open University Press.

MacIntyre, Alasdair (1981) *After Virtue*. London: Duckworth.

McIntyre, Donald (1997) The profession of educational research, *British Educational Research Journal*, 23(2), 127–40.

McLaren, Peter L. (1994) Postmodernism and the death of politics. In Peter L. McLaren and Colin Lankshear (eds) *Politics of Liberation: Paths from Freire*. London: Routledge.

MacLure, Maggie (1996) Telling transitions: boundary work in narratives of becoming an action researcher, *British Educational Research Journal*, 22(3), 273–86.

McTaggart, Robin (1994) Participative action research: issues in theory and practice, *Educational Action Research*, 2(3), 309–12.

McTaggart, Robin, Henry, Helen and Johnson, Evelyn (1997) Traces of participatory action research: reciprocity among educators, *Educational Action Research*, 5(1), 123–40.

Martin, Jane Roland (1994) *Changing the Educational Landscape: Philosophy, Women, and the Curriculum*. London: Routledge.

Midgley, Mary (1994) *The Ethical Primate: Humans, Freedom and Morality*. London: Routledge.

Miles, M. B. and Huberman, M. (1984) *Qualitative Data Analysis: an Expanded Sourcebook*. London: Sage.

Milgram, S. (1963) Behavioral study of obedience, *Journal of Abnormal and Social Psychology*, 67, 371–8.

Miller, David (1976) *Social Justice*. Oxford: Clarendon Press.

Mirza, Mehreen (1995) Some ethical dilemmas in field work: feminist and antiracist methodologies. In Morwenna Griffiths and Barry Troyna (eds) *Antiracism, Culture and Social Justice in Education*. Stoke-on-Trent: Trentham.

Morse, Janice M. (1994) Designing funded qualitative research. In N. K. Denzin and Y. S. Lincoln (eds) *Handbook of Qualitative Research*. London: Sage.

Myers, Kate (1990) Review of 'Equal Opportunities in the new ERA', *Education*, 5 October, 295.

Neal, Sarah (1995) Researching powerful people from an anti-racist and feminist perspective: a note on gender, collusion and marginality, *British Educational Research Journal*, 21(4), 517–31.

Norman, Richard (1995) No end to equality, *Journal of Philosophy of Education*, 29(3), 421–31.

O'Hanlon, Christine (1995) Editorial, *British Educational Research Journal Special Issue. Teacher Research: Methodological and Empowerment Issues in Practical Research for Improved Teaching and Learning*, 21(3), 259–61.

Opie, Anne (1992) Qualitative research: appropriation of the 'other' and empowerment, *Feminist Review*, 40 (Spring), 53–69.

Paechter, Carrie (1993) Power, knowledge and the design and technology curriculum. Unpublished PhD thesis, King's College, London.

Paechter, Carrie (1998) Investigating power in the staffroom: issues in the study of power and gender relations in a professional group, *Cambridge Journal of Education*, in the press.

Patai, Daphne (1994) When method becomes power. In Andrew Gitlin (ed.) *Power and Method: Political Activism and Educational Research*. London: Routledge.

Pateman, Carole (1988) *The Sexual Contract*. Cambridge: Polity Press.

Plato (1987) *The Republic*. Harmondsworth: Penguin.

Porter, Marilyn (1995) Second-hand ethnography: some problems in analysing a feminist project. In Alan Bryman and Robert Burgess (eds) *Analysing Qualitative Data*. London: Routledge.

Pryor, John (1995) Gender issues in group work – a case study involving work with computers, *British Educational Research Journal*, 21(3), 277–88.

Punch, Maurice (1994) Politics and ethics in qualitative research. In Norman K. Denzin and Yvonna S. Lincoln (eds) *Handbook of Qualitative Research*. London: Sage.

Rabinow, Paul (ed.) (1984) *The Foucault Reader.* Harmondsworth: Penguin.

Ranson, Stewart (1996) The future of educational research, *British Educational Research Journal,* 22(5), 532–6.

Raphael, D. D. (1976) *Problems of Political Philosophy.* London: Macmillan.

Rattansi, Ali (1992) Changing the subject? Racism, culture and education. In James Donald and Ali Rattansi (eds) *'Race' Culture and Difference.* London: Sage.

Rattansi, Ali (1995) Just framing: ethnicities and racisms in a 'postmodern' framework. In Linda Nicholson and Steven Seidman (eds) *Social Postmodernism.* Cambridge: Cambridge University Press.

Rawls, John (1972) *A Theory of Justice.* Oxford: Oxford University Press.

Richardson, Robin (1990) *Daring to Be a Teacher.* Stoke-on-Trent: Trentham.

Richardson, Robin (1996) *Fortunes and Fables: Education for Hope in Troubled Times.* Stoke-on-Trent: Trentham.

Riddell, Sheila (1989) Exploiting the exploited? The ethics of feminist educational research. In R. C. Burgess (ed.) *The Ethics of Educational Research.* London: Falmer Press.

Riddell, Sheila and Vincent, Carol (eds) (1997) Reflexive Accounts of Educational Reform, special issue of *British Educational Research Journal,* 23(3), 251–6.

Rieser, Richard and Mason, Micheline (1992) *Disability Equality in the Classroom: a Human Rights Issue.* London: Disability Equality in Education.

Robson, Colin (1993) *Real World Research: a Resource for Social Scientists and Practitioner-researchers.* Oxford: Blackwell.

Rogers, Marigold (1994) Growing up lesbian: the role of the school. In Debbie Epstein (ed.) *Challenging Lesbian and Gay Inequalities in Education.* Buckingham: Open University Press.

Rose, Hilary (1994) *Love, Power and Knowledge: towards a Feminist Transformation of the Sciences.* Cambridge: Polity Press.

Rosenthal, R. and Jacobson, L. (1968) *Pygmalion in the Classroom.* New York: Holt, Rinehart and Winston.

Rustin, Michael (1995) Equality in post-modern times. In David Miller and Michael Walzer (eds) *Pluralism, Justice, and Equality.* Oxford: Oxford University Press.

Said, Edward (1978) *Orientalism: Western Conceptions of the Orient.* Harmondsworth: Penguin.

Said, Edward (1993) *Culture and Imperialism.* London: Chatto and Windus.

Sandel, Michel (ed.) (1984) *Liberalism and Its Critics.* Oxford: Basil Blackwell.

Schön, Donald (1983) *The Reflective Practitioner.* London: Temple Smith.

Seller, Anne (1994) Should the feminist philosopher stay at home? In Kathleen Lennon and Margaret Whitford (eds) *Knowing the Difference: Feminist Perspectives in Epistemology.* London: Routledge.

Sewell, Tony (1996a) *Black Masculinities and Schooling: How Black Boys Survive Modern Schooling.* Stoke-on-Trent: Trentham.

Sewell, Tony (1996b) Values and validity: negotiations of power inside Black masculine research. Paper presented to British Educational Research Association Annual Conference, Lancaster University.

Siraj-Blatchford, Iram (1994) *Praxis Makes Perfect: Critical Educational Research for Social Justice.* Ticknall: Education Now Books.

Siraj-Blatchford, Iram and Siraj-Blatchford, John (1997) Reflexivity, social justice and educational research, *Cambridge Journal of Education,* 27(2), 235–48.

Skeggs, Beverley (1991) Postmodernism: what is all the fuss about?, *British Journal of Sociology of Education*, 12, 255–67.

Somekh, Bridget (1994) Inhabiting each other's castles: towards knowledge and mutual growth through collaboration, *Educational Action Research*, 2(3), 357–81.

Somekh, Bridget (1995) The contribution of action research to development in social endeavours: a position paper on action research methodology, *British Educational Research Journal*, 21(3), 339–55.

Soper, Kate (1993) Postmodernism, subjectivity and the question of value. In J. Squires (ed.) *Principled Positions: Postmodernity and the Rediscovery of Value*. London: Lawrence and Wishart.

Spender, Dale (1982) *Invisible Women: the Schooling Scandal*. London: Readers and Writers.

Spivak, Gayatri (1988) Can the subaltern speak? In Cary Nelson and Lawrence Grossberg (eds) *Marxism and the Interpretation of Culture*. Chicago: University of Illinois Press.

Spivak, Gayatri (1990) *The Post Colonial Critic: Interviews, Strategies, Dialogues*. London: Routledge.

Stanley, Liz (1990) *Feminist Praxis: Research, Theory and Epistemology in Feminist Sociology*. London: Routledge.

Stronach, Ian (1997) The educational polemics of Melanie Phillips, *Research Intelligence*, 60, 21–5.

Stronach, Ian, Allan, Julie and Morris, Brian (1996) Can the mothers of invention make virtue out of necessity? An optimistic deconstruction of research compromises in contract research and evaluation, *British Educational Research Journal*, 22(4), 493–509.

Stronach, Ian and MacLure, Maggie (1997) *Educational Research Undone*. Buckingham: Open University Press.

Taylor, Charles (1985) Interpretation and the sciences of man. In *Philosophy and the Human Sciences: Philosophical Papers 2*. Cambridge: Cambridge University Press.

Taylor, Charles (1989) *Sources of the Self*. Cambridge: Cambridge University Press.

Thompson, E. P. (1980) *Writing by Candlelight*. London: Merlin.

Troyna, Barry (1993) *Racism and Education: Research Perspectives*. Buckingham: Open University Press.

Troyna, Barry (1995) Blind faith? 'Empowerment' and educational research, *International Studies in Sociology of Education*, 4, 3–24.

Troyna, Barry and Carrington, Bruce (1989) Whose side are we on? Ethical dilemmas in research on 'race' and education. In Robert Burgess (ed.) *The Ethics of Educational Research*. London: Falmer Press.

Usher, Robin and Edwards, Richard (1994) *Postmodernism and Education*. London: Routledge.

Vincent, Carol (1996) *Parents and Teachers: Power and Participation*. London: Falmer Press.

Vincent, Carol and Tomlinson, Sally (1997) Home–school relationships: the swarming of disciplinary mechanisms, *British Educational Research Journal*, 23(3), 361–78.

Walford, Geoffrey (1991) Researching the City Technology College, Kingshurst. In Geoffrey Walford (ed.) *Doing Educational Research*. London: Routledge.

Walker, Melanie (1995) Context, critique and change: doing action research in South Africa, *Educational Action Research*, 3(1), 9–27.

Walker, Melanie (1996a) Subaltern professionals: acting in pursuit of social justice, *Educational Action Research*, 4(3), 407–25.

Walker, Melanie (1996b) Transgressing boundaries: everyday/academic discourses. In S. Hollingsworth (ed.) *International Action Research and Educational Reform*. London: Falmer Press.

Walkerdine, Valerie (1990) *Schoolgirl Fictions*. London: Verso.

Walzer, Michael (1983) *Spheres of Justice: a Defence of Pluralism and Equality*. Oxford: Blackwell.

Weiler, Kathleen (1994) Freire and a feminist pedagogy of difference. In Peter L. McLaren and Colin Lankshear (eds) *Politics of Liberation: Paths from Freire*. London: Routledge.

Weiner, Gaby (1989) Professional self-knowledge versus social justice: a critical analysis of the teacher-researcher movement, *British Educational Research Journal*, 15(1), 41–51.

Weiner, Gaby (1994) *Feminisms in Education*. Buckingham: Open University Press.

West, Cornell (1993) *Keeping Faith: Philosophy and Faith in America*. London: Routledge.

White, John (1994) The dishwasher's child: education and the end of egalitarianism, *Journal of Philosophy of Education*, 28(2), 173–81.

Whitehead, Jack (1993) *The Growth of Educational Knowledge: Creating Your Own Educational Theories*. Bournemouth: Hyde Publications.

Whitehead, Jack (1996) Researching educational inequality: a response to Poster and Hammersley, *Research Intelligence*, 56, 20–2.

Williams, Bernard (1973) *Problems of the Self: Philosophical Papers 1956–1972*. Cambridge: Cambridge University Press.

Williams, Patricia J. (1995) *The Rooster's Egg*. Cambridge, MA: Harvard University Press.

Williams, Raymond (1985) *Towards 2000*. Harmondsworth: Penguin.

Willis, Paul (1977) *Learning to Labour: How Working Class Kids Get Working Class Jobs*. Aldershot: Gower.

Wittgenstein, Ludwig (1968) *Philosophical Investigations*. Oxford: Blackwell.

Wright, Cecile (1986) School processes – an ethnographic study. In J. Eggleston, D. Dunn and M. Anjali (eds) *Education for Some*. Stoke-on-Trent: Trentham.

Wright, Cecile (1990) Comments in reply to the article by Peter Foster, *British Educational Research Journal*, 16(4), 351–5.

Yeatman, Anna (1994) Postmodern epistemological politics and social science. In Kathleen Lennon and Margaret Whitford (eds) *Knowing the Difference: Feminist Perspectives in Epistemology*. London: Routledge.

Index